80 PRACTICAL TIME-SAVING PROGRAMS FOR THE TRS-80

No. 1293
$15.95

80 PRACTICAL TIME-SAVING PROGRAMS FOR THE TRS-80

BY CHARLES J. CARROLL

TAB BOOKS Inc.
BLUE RIDGE SUMMIT, PA. 17214

FIRST EDITION

FIRST PRINTING

Library of Congress Cataloging in Publication Data

Carroll, Charles J.
    80 practical time-saving programs for the TRS-80.

    Includes index.
    1. TRS-80 (Computer)—Programming. 2. Computer pro-
grams. I. Title.   II. Title: Eighty practical time-saving programs for
the TRS-80.
QA76.8.T18C37   001.64′24   81-9276
ISBN 0-8306-0010-8   AACR2
ISBN 0-8306-1293-9 (pbk.)

Preface

This book has one purpose: to be a time saver. In all the time spent writing and debugging programs, one of the most frustrating occurences is to need a formula for the particular program at hand. More times than not, precious time is spent looking for that elusive formula or its derivation. In this book I've tried to put in one single place many different types of programs with the hope that they will provide the necessary information you seek. Needless to say, many of the programs were direct results of my own interests. However, I've tried to add others from different fields to provide a suitable cross section.

The biggest problem when writing this book was in hitting a happy medium between simple, mundane programs and more complicated, obscure ones. Ohms law, for instance, does not require a separate program. Its usage is wide enough that the formula should be at one's fingertips. In the same way that many of us have become dependent on the hand calculator (Quick: what's 15 × 12?), myself included, we should not let the computer rule our existence down to the smallest detail. Remember, the calculator is an excellent time saver, not a crutch. Therefore, in this book you will see some basic indentity-type programs as well as some complicated single-purpose programs. Each, though, has been selected to provide a source of information. With this information at your finger tips, you, too, will hopefully, have more time for using your computer.

Dedication

For My Very Organized Father
From His Very Disorganized Son:

"Time has value, and we each spend
that value for our own satisfactions."

Contents

1 Numbers   **11**
Polar/Rectangular Conversions—Complex Operations—
Complex Functions—Conversion to Base—Conversion From
Base 10—Simultaneous Equations—Numerical Integration

2 Finance   **30**
Compound Interest—Years of Interest—Interest Rate—Future
Value—Required Payment—Number of Payments I:—
Savings—Monthly Loan Payment—Loan Balance—Number
of Payments II: Loan—Loan Amount—Sinking Fund

3 Statistics   **54**
Permutations—Combinations—Arithmetic Mean—Geo-
metric Mean—Harmonic Mean—Grouped Data Mean—
Standard Deviation—Ungrouped Data—Standard Devia-
tion—Grouped Data—Linear Regression—Logrithmic Curve
Fit—Exponential Curve Fit—Factorial—Chi-Square Evaluation

4 Electronics   **91**
Antenna Patters—Gamma Match—Omega Match—T Pad—Pi
Pad—Minimum-Loss Pad—Parallel/Series Conversions—
Matching Networks—Capacitive-Divider Network—Series-
Matching Section—Microstrip

5 Geometry   **153**
Inverse Hyperbolic Functions—Complex Functions—
Complex Hyperbolic Functions—Triangles—Great Circle
Calculations

Appendix A   Statements and Commands in Basic   230

Appendix B   Powers of Two   236

Appendix C   Hexadecimal-Decimal Integer Conversion 237

Index   249

List of Programs

Numbers
Polar/Rectangular Conversion 12
Complex Operations 14
Complex Functions 17
Conversion to Base 10 19
Conversion from Base 10 21
Simultaneous Equations 24
Numerical Integrations 26

Finance
Compound Interest 31
Years of Interest 33
Interest Rate 35
Future Value 37
Required Payment 39
Number of Payments - Savings 41
Monthly Loan Payment 43
Loan Balance 45
Number of Payments - Loan 48
Loan Amount 50
Sinking Fund 52

Statistics
Permutations 55
Combinations 57
Arithmetic Mean 59
Geometric Mean 61
Harmonic Mean 63
Grouped Data Mean 65
Standard Deviation - Ungrouped Data 69
Standard Deviation - Grouped Data 71
Linear Regression 73
Logrithmic Curve Fit 78
Exponential Curve Fit 81
Factorial 87
Chi-Square Evaluation 89

Electronics

Antenna Pattern	93
Gamma Match	101
Omega Match	109
T/pad	117
Pi/pad	120
Minimum Loss-Pad	123
Parallel/Series Conversions	125
Matching Networks A, B, C, D	128
Capacitive-DividerNetwork	143
Series-Matching Section	147
Microstrip	151

Geometry

Hyperbolic Functions - Sine, Cosine, Tangent, Cotangent, Secant Cosecant	154
Six Inverse Hyperbolic Functions	168
Six Complex Functions	181
Six Inverse Complex Functions	180
Six Complex Hyperbolic Functions	207
Four Triangles	218
Great Circle Calculations	228

Chapter 1
Numbers

This chapter contains only seven different programs, but each program is useful in many different ways. The first three programs form the basis for many others, since complex operations and polar/rectangular conversions are used in many different facets of electronics. And, needless to say, where else do you find different bases but in computers?

I've tried to present the programs in such an order that the basic programs are first, followed by the more complex programs which may, or may not, use parts of the basic programs. In this way the later programs will be easier to understand, and you should be able to pull parts out as your own needs dictate.

POLAR/RECTANGULAR CONVERSION

The polar/rectangular conversion is one of the most fundamental programs around. However, as with most of the other programs in this book, it's not one that you can recite without some extra time for thought. Figure 1-1 shows a diagram that relates the various components of the conversions.

To convert from polar to rectangular use the following equations:

$$X = McosT$$
$$Y = McosT$$

where M is the magnitude and T is the angle in the polar notation. For rectangular to polar, use:

$$M = \sqrt{X^2 + Y^2}$$
$$T = \arctan(Y/X)$$

Polar/Rectangular Conversion Program

```
5 'P/R CONVERSION
10 CLS
20 PRINT"SELECT APPROPRIATE FUNCTI
   ON  P"CHR$(94)"R (1) OR  R"CHR$
   (94)"P (2)"
30 INPUT N
40 IF N=1 PRINT"ENTER MAGNITUDE, P
   HASE ANGLE":INPUT M,T ELSE GOTO
   80
50 X=M*COS(T*.01745329)
60 Y=M*SIN(T*.01745329)
70 PRINT"X="X" AND  Y="Y:END
80 PRINT"ENTER X AND Y":INPUT X,Y
90 M=SQR(X↑2+Y↑2)
100 T=ATN(Y/X)*57.29578
110 PRINT"MAGNITUDE="M "AND PHASE
    ANGLE="T
```

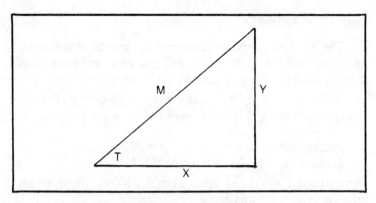

Fig. 1-1. How the various components of polar/rectangular conversions relate to each other.

Sample Program

SELECT APPROPRIATE FUNCTION P ⬧ R(1) OR R ⬧ P(2)
? 1
ENTER MAGNITUDE, PHASE ANGLE
? 3, 60
X = 1.5 AND Y = 2.59808
SELECT APPROPRIATE FUNCTION P⬧R (1) OR R⬧P (2)
? 2
ENTER X AND Y
? 5, 12
MAGNITUDE = 13 AND PHASE ANGLE = 67.3802

COMPLEX OPERATIONS

The complex operations comprise the four basic arithmetic functions: addition, subtraction, multiplication and division of complex numbers. The equations for the functions are:

addition - $(x_1 + iy_1) + (x_2 + iy_2) = (x_1 + x_2) + (y_1 + y_2)\,i$

subtraction - $(x_1 + iy_1 + (x_2 + iy_2) = (x_1 + x_2) + (y_1 + y_2)\iota$

$- (x_2 - (y_1 + iy_1)$

multiplication - $(x_1 + iy_1)(x_2 + iy_2) = M_1/M_2\,T_1$

division - $(x_1 + iy_1)/(x_2 + iy_2) = M_1/M_2$

where M and T are the respective magnitudes and phase angles from the rectangular to polar conversion.

Complex Operation Program

```
5 'COMPLEX OPERATIONS
10 CLS
20 PRINT"SELECT THE APPROPRIATE CO
   MPLEX OPERATION"CHR$(13)TAB(20)
   "ADDITION            1"CHR$(13)TA
   B(20)"SUBTRACTION         2"CHR$(
   13)TAB(20)"MULTIPLICATION      3"
   CHR$(13)TAB(20)"DIVISION
      4"
30  INPUT N
40 PRINT"ENTER FIRST COMPLEX NUMBE
   R (REAL, IMAGINARY)":INPUT FR,F
   I
50 PRINT"ENTER SECOND COMPLEX NUMB
   ER (REAL, IMAGINARY)":INPUT SR,
   SI
60 IF N=1 GOTO 190
65 IF N=2 GOTO 170
70 FM=SQR(FR↑2+FI↑2)
80 FT=ATN(FI/FR)*57.29578
90 SM=SQR(SR↑2+SI↑2)
100 ST=ATN(SI/SR)*57.29578:IF N=3
    GOTO 150
110 AR=FM/SM
120 AI=FT-ST
130 BR=AR*COS(AI*.01745329)
140 BI=AR*SIN(AI*.01745329):GOTO 2
    10
```

```
150 AR=FM*SM
160 AI=FT+ST:GOTO 130
170 BR=FR-SR
180 BI=FI-SI:GOTO 210
190 BR=FR+SR
200 BI=FI+SI:GOTO 210
210 PRINT"ANSWER (REAL, IMAGINARY)
    -- "BR;BI
```

Complex Operation Sample Program

SELECT THE APPROPRIATE COMPLEX OPERATION

ADDITION	1
SUBTRACTION	2
MULTIPLICATION	3
DIVISION	4

? 3
ENTER FIRST COMPLEX NUMBER (REAL, IMAGINARY)
? 3,5
ENTER SECOND COMPLEX NUMBER (REAL, IMAGINARY)
? 6,– 9
ANSWER (REAL, IMAGINARY)
- - 63 3.0
SELECT THE APPROPRIATE COMPLEX OPERATION

ADDITION	1
SUBTRACTION	2
MULTIPLICATION	3
DIVISION	4

? 4
ENTER FIRST COMPLEX NUMBER (REAL, IMAGINARY)
? – 12, 3
ENTER SECOND COMPLEX NUMBER (REAL, IMAGINARY)
? 4, – 5
ANSWER (REAL, IMAGINARY)
- - 1.53658 1.17073

These two samples, multiplication and division, are the more difficult. They use the previous polar/rectangular conversion.

COMPLEX FUNCTIONS

The four complex functions—absolute value, square, reciprocal, and square root—also use the polar/rectangular conversion. The respective formulas are:

$$\text{absolute value} - |x| = M$$
$$\text{square} - x^2 = M^2 \underline{/2T}$$
$$\text{reciprocal} - \frac{1}{x} = \frac{1}{M} \underline{/-T}$$
$$\text{square root} = \sqrt{x} = \pm (\sqrt{M} \underline{/T/2})$$

with M and T the magnitude and phase angle from the rectangular/polar conversion.

Complex Function Program

```
5 'COMPLEX FUNCTIONS
10 CLS
20 PRINT"SELECT THE APPROPRIATE CO
   MPLEX OPERATION"CHR$(13)TAB(20)
   "ABSOLUTE VALUE      1"CHR$(13)TA
   B(20)"SQUARE              2"CHR$(
   13)TAB(20)"RECIPROCAL          3"
   CHR$(13)TAB(20)"SQUARE ROOT
      4"
30  INPUT N
40 PRINT"ENTER COMPLEX NUMBER (REA
   L, IMAGINARY)":INPUT R,I
50 M=SQR(R↑2+I↑2)
60 T=ATN(I/R)*57.29578
70 IF N=1 PRINT"ANSWER -- "M:END E
   LSE IF N=2 GOTO 120 ELSE IF N=3
    GOTO 100
80 AR=SQR(M)*COS(T/2*.01745329)
90 AI=SQR(M)*SIN(T/2*.01745329):
   GOTO 140
100 AR=1/M*COS(-T*.01745329)
110 AI=1/M*SIN(-T*.01745329):GOTO
    140
120 AR=R↑2*COS(2*T*.01745329)
130 AI=R↑2*SIN(2*T**01745329):GOTO
    140
140 PRINT"ANSWER (REAL, IMAGINARY)
    --"AR,AI
```

Complex Function Samples

SELECT THE APPROPRIATE COMPLEX FUNCTION

ABSOLUTE VALUE	1
SQUARE	2
RECIPROCAL	3
SQUARE ROOT	4

? 2
ENTER COMPLEX NUMBER (REAL, IMAGINARY)
2, −3
ANSWER (REAL, IMAGINARY) −−5.0 −12.0
SELECT THE APPROPRIATE COMPLEX FUNCTION

ABSOLUTE VALUE	1
SQUARE	2
RECIPROCAL	3
SQUARE ROOT	4

? 4
ENTER COMPLEX NUMBER (REAL, IMAGINARY)
? −3. 5, 7
ANSWER (REAL, IMAGINARY) −− 2.37973 −1.47076

CONVERSION TO BASE 10

In this program, which converts a number to base 10, I've actually treated the number as a string and then operated on each integer individually. For example, the first of four digits is multiplied by the base to the third power (1234_3 -- 1×3^3, 2×3^2, 3×3^1, and $4 \times 3^0 = 58$). The basic equation is: $N_{10} = X_n B^{n-1} + X_{n-1} B^{n-2} + X_{n-2} B^{n-3} \ldots X_2 B + X$

Conversion to Base 10 Program

```
5 'BASE CONVERSIONS
10 CLS
20 INPUT "ENTER NUMBER TO BE CONVE
   RTED TO BASE TEN";X#
25 INPUT "ENTER BASE OF NUMBER TO
   BE CONVERTED";B
30 N=LEN(STR$(X#))-1
35 M=N-1
40 FOR Q=2 TO N
50 S=S+VAL(MID$(STR$(X#),Q,1))*B↑M
55 M=M-1
60 NEXT Q
70 S=S+VAL(MID$(STR$(X#),Q,1))
80 PRINTX#"BASE"B"EQUALS"S"BASE TE
   N"
```

Base 10 Conversion Samples

ENTER NUMBER TO BE CONVERTED TO BASE TEN
? 3456
ENTER BASE OF NUMBER TO BE CONVERTED
? 7
3456 BASE 7 EQUALS 1266 BASE TEN
ENTER NUMBER TO BE CONVERTED TO BASE TEN
? 8776
ENTER BASE OF NUMBER TO BE CONVERTED
? 9
8776 BASE 9 EQUALS 6468 BASE TEN

CONVERSION FROM BASE 10

As with the previous program, the conversion from base 10 to a new base is handled by treating the individual digits as part of a string. Each digit is separated from the string and operated on with the new base and its appropriate exponent. A FOR NEXT loop is used to evaluate the entire number. During the loop, the individual digits are again stored in a string until the completion of the process.

A number is changed to a new base by the following equation:

$$N_x = X - I_{n-1}B^{n-1} - I_{n-2}B^{n-2} \ldots I_nB^n$$

Conversion From Base 10 Program

```
5 'BASE CONVERSION
10 CLS
12 CLEAR 1000
15 P=1
25 DIM Z$(300)
30 INPUT "ENTER THE NUMBER TO BE C
   ONVERTED (BASE 10)";N
40 M=N
50 INPUT "ENTER NEW BASE";B
60 FOR I=0 TO 50
70 X=INT(B↑I)
80 IF X>N GOTO 100
90 NEXT I
100 J=I
110 I=I-1
120 R=1
130 M=INT(M-INT(B↑I))
140 IF M=0 Z$(P)=STR$(R): GOTO 220
145 IF M=INT(B↑I)  GOTO 160
150 IF M<INT(B↑I)  GOTO 180
160 R=R+1:GOTO 130
180 Z$(P)=STR$(R):PRINTZ$(P)
190 P=P+1
200 I=I-1
210 IF M>=INT(B↑I) GOTO 120 ELSE R
    =0:GOTO 180
220 IF I=0 GOTO 250
230 FOR X=P+1 TO J
```

```
240 Z$(X)=STR$(A)
245 NEXT X
250 FOR Y=1 TO J
260 W$=W$+Z$(Y)
270 NEXT Y
280 PRINTN;"BASE 10 ="W$" BASE";B
```

New Base Conversion Samples

ENTER THE NUMBER TO BE CONVERTED (BASE 10)
? 3112
ENTER NEW BASE
? 7
1
2
0
3
3112 BASE 10 = 12034 BASE 7
ENTER THE NUMBER TO BE CONVERTED (BASE 10)
? 1234
ENTER NEW BASE
? 2
1
0
0
1
1
0
1
0
0
1234 BASE 10 = 10011010010 BASE 2

SIMULTANEOUS EQUATIONS

Use of this program will allow you to solve for two unknowns. Each of the unknowns is independently solved by using the coefficients of the terms in a matrix. Should the coefficients $A \cdot E - B \cdot D = 0$, the program will indicate a / $\emptyset$ error. This indicates that either no solution or a unique solution exists. To solve for X and Y, the following equations are used:

$$X = \frac{\begin{vmatrix} C & B \\ E & D \end{vmatrix}}{\begin{vmatrix} A & B \\ D & E \end{vmatrix}} = \frac{CE - BF}{AE - BD} \qquad Y = \frac{\begin{vmatrix} A & C \\ D & E \end{vmatrix}}{\begin{vmatrix} A & B \\ D & E \end{vmatrix}} = \frac{AF - DC}{AE - BD}$$

Simultaneous Equations Programs

```
5  'SIMULTANEOUS EQUATIONS
10 CLS
20 PRINT"TO SOLVE SIMULTANEOUS EQU
   ATIONS FOR TWO UNKNOWNS,"CHR$(1
   3)"REARRANGE THE EQUATIONS INTO
   THE FOLLOWING FORMAT."CHR$(1
   3)TAB(20)"AX+BY=C"CHR$(13)TAB(2
   0)"DX+EY=F"
30 INPUT"ENTER THE COEFFICIENTS --
   A,B,C,D,E,F";A,B,C,D,E,F
40 X=(C*E-B*F)/(A*E-B*D)
50 Y=(A*F-D*C)/(A*E-B*D)
60 PRINT"X="X"AND Y="Y
```

Simultaneous Equations Examples

In the following examples, the program will be used to solve for X and Y in the two groups of equations:

$$2X + 3Y = -5 \quad \text{and} \quad 9.5X - 8.5Y = 3$$
$$-5X - 2Y = 4 \qquad\qquad 2X + 4Y = -5$$

TO SOLVE SIMULTANEOUS EQUATIONS FOR TWO UN-KNOWNS,
REARRANGE THE EQUATIONS INTO THE FOLLOWING FORMAT.

$$AX + BY = C$$
$$DX + EY = F$$

ENTER THE COEFFICIENTS -- A,B,C,D,E,F,
? 2,3,-5,-5,-2,4
X = -.181818 AND Y = -1.54545
As proof:

$$2.-.181818 + 3.-1.54545 = -5$$
$$-5 \cdot -.181818 - 2 \cdot -1.54545 = 4$$

For the second equation:
TO SOLVE SIMULTANEOUS EQUATIONS FOR TWO UN-KNOWNS,
REARRANGE THE EQUATIONS INTO THE FOLLOWING FORMAT.

$$AX + BY = C$$
$$DX + EY = F$$

ENTER THE COEFFICIENTS -- A,B,C,D,E,F,
? 9.5, -8.5,3,2,3,-5
X = -.554546 AND Y = -.972727
As proof: $9.5 \cdot -.554546 - 8 \cdot - .972727 = 3$
$$2 \cdot -.554546 + 4 \cdot -.972727 = -5$$

NUMERICAL INTEGRATION

This program for numerical integration provides an easy and convenient way to solve the common integral calculus problem. One especially useful case is to solve for the area under a curve. In fact, by solving for the area bounded by the curve which describes an antenna directivity pattern, the gain of that antenna can be calculated.

In this program you must use an odd number of points, and the points must be equally spaced. If data is not available for equally spaced points, try using one of the curve fitting programs to determine the equation of the line bounding the area. From this equation, equally spaced points can be selected and solved to provide data for the numerical integration.

The actual integration is solved by use of Simpson's Rule which is:

$$\int_{x_0}^{x_n} f(x) \, dx \cong \frac{S}{3}$$

$$[f(x_0) + 4f(x_1) + 2f(x_2) \ldots 2f(x_{n-2}) + 4f(x_{n-1}) + f(x_n)]$$

Numerical Integration Program

```
5 'NUMERICAL INTEGRATION
10 CLS
15 DIMV$(100)
20 PRINT"ENTER THE SPACING BETWEEN
   THE SELECTED POINTS.  AN ODD"CH
   R$(13)"NUMBER OF POINTS MUST BE
   USED."
25 INPUT S:S=S/3
30 PRINT"ENTER THE VALUE FOR A SEL
   ECTED POINT.  USE A / TO DENOTE
   "CHR$(13)"THE END OF DATA."
40 FOR I=1 TO 100
50 INPUT V$(I)
55 IF V$(I)="/"GOTO80
60 V(I)=VAL(V$(I))
65 Q=Q+1
70 NEXT I
80 NI=S*V(1)+S*V(Q)
90 FOR I=2 TO Q-1STEP2
100 A=A+V(I)*S*4
```

```
110 NEXT I
120 FOR I=3 TO Q-2 STEP 2
130 B=B+V(I)*S*2
140 NEXT I
150 NI=NI+A+B
160 PRINT"ANSWER --"NI
```

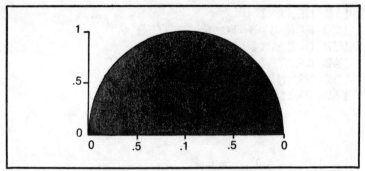

Fig. 1-2. The area (under the curve) which can be solved by using the 1st sample program for the numerical integration program.

Numerical Integration Sample Problems

This first problem (see Fig. 1-2) will solve for the area under the indicated curve. The greater the number of points used, the more accurate the answer.

ENTER THE SPACING BETWEEN THE SELECTED POINTS.
AN ODD NUMBER OF POINTS MUST BE USED.
? .314159
ENTER THE VALUE FOR A SELECTED POINT. USE A / TO
DENOTE THE END OF DATA.
? 0
? .0955
? .3455
? .6545
? .9045
? 1.0000
? .9045
? .6545
? .3455
? .0955
? 0
? /
ANSWER -- 1.5708

If the program were set up for double precision, the actual answer would be 1.570794939994812. To see the difference in answer accuracy, the next example will be run using seven instead of eleven points.

ENTER THE SPACING BETWEEN THE SELECTED POINTS.
AN ODD NUMBER OF POINTS MUST BE USED.
? .523598

ENTER THE VALUE FOR A SELECTED POINT. USE A / TO
DENOTE THE END OF DATA.
? 0
? .25
? .6545
? 1
? .6545
? .25
? 0
ANSWER -- 1.5704

With double precision, the answer is 1.570412255525589.
The actual difference in answers is very small, but it is used to
illustrate that the number of points will influence the final answer.

And finally, since the area under the curve is really a semicir-
cle, the actual answer is 1.570796327.

Chapter 2
Finance

The following chapter focuses on financial programs and deals with three main areas: loans, savings, and compounded interest. In each case, we're generally concerned with what any payment might be, how much time or number of payments required, and total value.

The most basic programs deal with compounded amounts/interest. The main variables in the different equations are: initial deposit (A), interest rate (I), future value (V), number of years (T) and number of times the principal is compounded per year (TY). Equations for the following programs are:

$$V = A \cdot (1 + I/TY) \blacklozenge (TY \cdot T)$$
$$T = \log\left(\frac{V}{A}\right) / \log\left(1 + I/TY\right) \cdot TY$$
$$I = \left(\left[\frac{V}{A}\right]\right)^{\dfrac{1}{T \cdot TY}} - 1) \cdot TY$$

COMPOUND INTEREST

This program will compute the final amount after some initial principal has been compounded periodically, *with no further deposits*. Additional deposit programs will be shown later in this chapter.

Compound Interest Program

```
5 'COMPOUND INTEREST
10 CLS
20 INPUT "ENTER AMOUNT TO BE COMPO
   UNDED";A
30 INPUT "ENTER INTEREST RATE";I:I
   =I/100
40 INPUT "ENTER NUMBER OF YEARS MO
   NEY IS COMPOUNDED";T
50 INPUT "ENTER NUMBER OF COMPOUND
   PERIODS PER YEAR";TY
62 V=A*(1+I/TY)^(TY*T)
70 PRINT"$"INT(V*100+.5)/100
```

Sample Compound Interest Problems

In these problems, the interest rate is entered as a percentage number rather than a decimal, i.e., 6 percent instead of 0.06. What will be the value of $1500 in 9 years if it is deposited at 7.5 percent (year interest rate) and compounded quarterly?

```
ENTER AMOUNT TO BE COMPOUNDED
? 1500
ENTER INTEREST RATE
? 7.5
ENTER NUMBER OF YEARS MONEY IS COMPOUNDED
? 9
ENTER NUMBER OF COMPOUND PERIODS PER YEAR
? 4
$ 2927.69
```

After $15,000 is deposited for 20 years at 5.5 percent yearly interest (compounded semi-annually), what will be the total value of the principal?

```
ENTER AMOUNT TO BE COMPOUNDED
? $15,000
ENTER INTEREST RATE
? 5.5
ENTER NUMBER OF YEARS MONEY IS COMPOUNDED
? 20
ENTER NUMBER OF COMPOUND PERIODS PER YEAR
? 2
$ 44,298
```

YEARS OF INTEREST

This program deals with the number of years some principal will have to remain on deposit to reach a specific value.

Years of Interest Program

```
5 'NO.YEARS OF COMPOUND INTEREST
10 CLS
20 INPUT "ENTER AMOUNT TO BE COMPO
   UNDED";A
30 INPUT "ENTER INTeREST RATE";I:I
   =I/100
40 INPUT "ENTER FINAL DESIRED AMOU
   NT";V
50 INPUT "ENTER NUMBER OF COMPOUND
   PERIODS PER YEAR";TY
60 T=LOG(V/A)/((LOG(1+I/TY))*TY)
70 PRINT"COMPOUNDED"TY"TIMES PER Y
   EAR WILL REQUIRE THE MONEY TO B
   E DEPOSITED"INT(T*10+.5)/10"YEA
   RS"
```

Sample Problems

How many years will $1000 dollars have to remain on deposit if the interest rate is 9.5 percent, the money is compounded quarterly, and the final desired amount is $2000?

ENTER AMOUNT TO BE COMPOUNDED
? 1000
ENTER INTEREST RATE
? 9.5
ENTER FINAL DESIRED AMOUNT
? 2000
ENTER NUMBER OF COMPOUND PERIODS PER YEAR
? 4
COMPOUNDED 4 TIMES PER YEAR WILL REQUIRE
THE MONEY TO BE DEPOSITED 7.4 YEARS.

If the annual inflation rate averages 10 percent, in how many years will the price of some item double? For this problem assume that the price is currently $100 and will double to $200.
ENTER THE AMOUNT TO BE COMPOUNDED
? 100

ENTER INTEREST RATE
? 10
ENTER FINAL DEPOSITED AMOUNT
? 200
ENTER NUMBER OF COMPOUND PERIODS PER YEAR
? 1
COMPOUNDED 1 TIME PER YEAR WILL REQUIRE THE
MONEY TO BE DEPOSITED 7.3 YEARS.

Or, in other words, with an annual inflation rate of 10 percent, prices will double every 7.3 years!

INTEREST RATE

With the many different types of savings instruments available, a person often has to evaluate each instrument versus his particular needs. This program is designed to calculate the amount of interest required to attain some final amount of money. This is especially useful with the varying amounts of time required by different savings plans. Note that the interest rate can also be considered as a rate of return for some initial deposit or investment.

Interest Rate Program

```
5 'RATE OF RETURN
10 CLS
20 INPUT "ENTER AMOUNT TO BE COMPO
   UNDED";A
30 INPUT "ENTER FINAL AMOUNT";V
40 INPUT "ENTER NUMBER OF YEARS MO
   NEY IS COMPOUNDED";T
50 INPUT "ENTER NUMBER OF COMPOUND
   PERIODS PER YEAR";TY
60 I=((V/A)^(1/(TY*T))-1)*TY
70 PRINT"RATE OF RETURN IS"I*100"P
   ERCENT PER YEAR"
```

Sample Interest Rate Problems

What interest rate is required to double your money in 2 years?

ENTER AMOUNT TO BE COMPOUNDED
? 1
ENTER FINAL AMOUNT
? 2
ENTER NUMBER OF YEARS MONEY IS COMPOUNDED
? 2
ENTER NUMBER OF COMPOUND PERIODS PER YEAR
? 1
RATE OF RETURN IS 41.4214 PERCENT PER YEAR

Obviously, doubling your money requires a high rate of return, a rate that is not available through normal savings interest. Therefore, to double your money in a short period of time requires a more speculative type of investment, one that causes the chances of losing your money to increase in proportion to the rate of return.

You wish to make an initial deposit of $5000 into a college education fund which will yield $25000 in 15 years. If the money is compounded quarterly, what rate of return must the fund yield per year?

ENTER AMOUNT TO BE COMPOUNDED
? 5000
ENTER FINAL AMOUNT
? 25000
ENTER NUMBER OF YEARS MONEY IS COMPOUNDED
? 15
ENTER NUMBER OF COMPOUND PERIODS PER YEAR
? 4
RATE OF RETURN IS 10.8748 PERCENT PER YEAR

FUTURE VALUE

This group of programs deals with the same basic savings theme, though with periodic payments made into some savings instrument. First, the most basic: what is the future value of X dollars deposited Y times at Z interest? The equation for this computation is:

Future Value Program

$$FV = \frac{A}{I} ((1+I)^{T+1} - (1+I))$$

```
5 'FUTURE VALUE
10 CLS
20 INPUT "ENTER AMOUNT OF MONTHLY
   DEPOSIT";A
30 INPUT "ENTER INTEREST RATE";I:I
   =I/1200
40 INPUT "ENTER NUMBER OF YEARS";T
   :T=T*12
50 FV=A/I*((1+I)^(T+1)-(1+I))
60 PRINT"$"INT(FV*100+.5)/100
```

Sample Future Value Problems

How much money will a person have if he deposits $200 each month for 10 years? The interest rate is 6 percent per year.
ENTER AMOUNT OF MONTHLY DEPOSIT
? 200
ENTER INTEREST RATE
? 6
ENTER NUMBER OF YEARS
? 10
$ 32939.60

Note that the actual money deposited was $24000 ($2400/ year for 10 years).

REQUIRED PAYMENT

The next program deals with the required deposit each month to attain some specific goal. This is extremely useful when trying to determine how much money is available from a budget for the purchase of some article, i.e., a car payment. To determine the monthly payment, use the following equation:

$$A = \frac{FV \cdot I}{(1+I)^{T+1} - (1+I)}$$

Required Payment Program

```
5 'PAYMENT FOR AMOUNT
10 CLS
20 INPUT "ENTER FINAL DESIRED AMOU
   NT";FV
30 INPUT "ENTER INTEREST RATE";I:I
   =I/1200
40 INPUT "ENTER NUMBER OF YEARS";T
   :T=T*12
50 A=(FV*I)/(((1STEPRETURNSONLEFT$
```

Sample Payment Problems

You will need $15000 in 7 years. How large a monthly payment do you need if the annual interest rate is 8.5 percent?

ENTER FINAL DESIRED AMOUNT
? 15000
ENTER INTEREST RATE
? 8.5
ENTER NUMBER OF YEARS
? 7
$ 130.38 MONTHLY PAYMENTS

A new car costs $7000. What is the monthly payment over 4 years if the interest rate is 12.5 percent? Disregard any interest payments.

ENTER FINAL DESIRED AMOUNT
? 7000
ENTER INTEREST RATE
? 12.5
ENTER NUMBER OF YEARS
? 4
$ 111.98 MONTHLY PAYMENTS

This amount is necessary to pay off the principal in 4 years. As you'll see later in this chapter, the amount required for interest payments raises the monthly payment considerably.

NUMBER OF PAYMENTS I: SAVINGS

The final program in this group of three (Future Value and Required Payment are the other two) will determine the number of equal payments necessary to achieve some final amount. As before, you will enter the monthly deposit, the total desired amount, and the interest rate.

To solve for the number of payments, use the following equation:

$$N = \frac{\log\left(\dfrac{V \cdot I}{A} + 1 + I\right)}{\log(1 + I)}$$

Number of Payments Program

```
5 'NUMBER OF PAYMENTS
10 CLS
20 INPUT "ENTER AMOUNT TO BE FINANC
   ED";P
30 INPUT "ENTER INTEREST RATE IN P
   ERCENT";I:I=I/1200
40 INPUT "ENTER AMOUNT OF AFFORDAB
   LE MONTHLY PAYMENT";A
50 N=LOG(A/(A-P*I))/LOG(1+I)
60 PRINTN"MONTHLY PAYMENTS"
```

Sample Payments Program

How long will it take to save $1200 if you are making monthly payments of $15 at 10 percent interest?

ENTER AMOUNT OF MONTHLY PAYMENT
? 15
ENTER INTEREST RATE
? 10
ENTER FINAL AMOUNT
? 1200
$ 1200 WILL REQUIRE DEPOSITS OF $ 15 FOR 61.1569 MONTHS

You make quarterly deposits of $450 into a savings account. If the interest rate is 7.5 percent, how many months will it take to accumulate $15000 in the account?

ENTER AMOUNT OF MONTHLY DEPOSIT
? 150 (450/3)
ENTER INTEREST RATE
? 7.5
ENTER FINAL AMOUNT
? 15000
$ 15000 WILL REQUIRE DEPOSITS OF $150 FOR 77.5398 MONTHS
(Or, quarterly deposits for 6.5 years)

MONTHLY LOAN PAYMENT

This program will calculate the total monthly loan payment given the amount, interest rate, and number of payments. The program is based on:

$$A = P \left[\frac{I/12}{1-(1-I/12)^{-N}} \right]$$

Loan Payment Program

```
5 'MONTHLY LOAN PAYMENT
10 CLS
20 INPUT "ENTER AMOUNT TO BE FINAN
   CED";P
30 INPUT "ENTER INTEREST RATE IN P
   ERCENT";I:I=I/100
40 INPUT "ENTER NUMBER OF YEARS OF
   FINANCING";N:N=N*12
50 A=P*(I/12)/(1-(1+(I/12))↑-N)
60 PRINT"MONTHLY PAYMENT IS $"INT(
   A*100+.5)/100
```

Loan Payment Program Examples

A new car costs $7000. What is the monthly payment over 4 years if the interest rate is 12.5 percent?

ENTER AMOUNT TO BE FINANCED
? 7000
ENTER INTEREST RATE IN PERCENT
? 12.5
ENTER NUMBER OF YEARS OF FINANCING
? 4
MONTHLY PAYMENT IS $186.06

You'll note that this is considerably above the $112 payment. Payment for the interest amounts to about two-thirds of the principal payment.

LOAN BALANCE

This section deals with the balance on a loan financed over some period of time. As demonstrated in the previous example (Monthly Loan Payment), payments on the interest are a significant portion of a monthly payment. In fact, in the case of a home mortgage, the interest payment is virtually the entire payment for the first several years. This Loan Payment program is designed to show the principal balance and accumulated interest after a desired number of payments. With this information, you can generate a schedule of interest paid, a number that is used when computing your Federal Income Tax return.

To compute the balance and interest, use:

$$B = \frac{1}{(1+I)^{-y}} \left[A \cdot \frac{(1+I)^{-y} - 1}{I} + P \right]$$

$$AI = B_y - B_{x-1} + (y - X + 1) A$$

Loan Balance Program

```
5 'LOAN BALANCE
10 CLS
20 INPUT "ENTER AMOUNT TO BE FINAN
   CED";P
30 INPUT "ENTER INTEREST RATE IN P
   ERCENT";I:I=I/1200
40 INPUT "ENTER MONTHLY PAYMENT";A
50 INPUT "ENTER BEGINNING PAYMENT
   NUMBER";X
60 INPUT "ENTER ENDING PAYMENT NUM
   BER";Y
70 B=1/((I+1)↑-Y)*((A*(((1+I)↑-Y)-
   1))/I+P)
80 PRINT"BALANCE AT THE END OF PAY
   MENT NUMBER"Y"-- $"INT(B*100+.5
   )/100
90 AI=B-(1/((I+1)↑-(X-1))*((A*(((1
   +I)↑-(X-1))-1))/I+P))+(Y-X+1)*A
100 PRINT"ACCUMULATED INTEREST AT
    THE END OF PAYMENT NUMBER"Y"--
    $"INT(AI*100+.5)/100
```

Sample Loan Balance Problems

A $40000 mortgage is arranged such that the first payment is in January. The mortgage is 9 percent over 30 years and the payment is $321.85 (use the previous program for Monthly Loan Payment to compute the payment). Determine the interest paid after the first, fifth, twentieth, and thirtieth year.

ENTER AMOUNT TO BE FINANCED
? 40000
ENTER INTEREST RATE IN PERCENT
? 9
ENTER MONTHLY PAYMENT
? 321.85
ENTER BEGINNING PAYMENT NUMBER
? 1
ENTER ENDING PAYMENT NUMBER
? 12 (12th month)
BALANCE AT THE END OF PAYMENT NUMBER 12 — $39726.70
ACCUMULATED INTEREST AT THE END OF PAYMENT NUMBER 12 — $3588.92

ENTER AMOUNT TO BE FINANCED
? 40000
ENTER INTEREST RATE IN PERCENT
? 9
ENTER MONTHLY PAYMENT
? 321.85
ENTER BEGINNING PAYMENT NUMBER
? 49
ENTER ENDING PAYMENT NUMBER
? 60
BALANCE AT THE END OF PAYMENT NUMBER 60 — $38352
ACCUMULATED INTEREST AT THE END OF PAYMENT NUMBER 60 — $3471.02

The total amount paid per year on the mortgage is $3862.20. So even at the end of the fifth year, almost 90 percent of the monthly payment is still going for interest payments. However, look at the situation in the fifteenth and twentieth years:

ENTER AMOUNT TO BE FINANCED
? 40000
ENTER INTEREST RATE IN PERCENT
? 9

ENTER MONTHLY PAYMENT
? 321.85
ENTER BEGINNING PAYMENT NUMBER
? 169
ENTER ENDING PAYMENT NUMBER
? 180
BALANCE AT THE END OF PAYMENT NUMBER 180 —
$31732.10
ACCUMULATED INTEREST AT THE END OF PAYMENT
NUMBER 180 — $2903.31

ENTER AMOUNT TO BE FINANCED
? 40000
ENTER INTEREST RATE IN PERCENT
? 9
ENTER MONTHLY PAYMENT
? 321.85
ENTER BEGINNING PAYMENT NUMBER
? 229
ENTER ENDING PAYMENT NUMBER
? 240
BALANCE AT THE END OF PAYMENT NUMBER 240 —
$25407.30
ACCUMULATED INTEREST AT THE END OF PAYMENT
NUMBER 240 — $2360.87

Even at the end of the twentieth year, more than 60 percent of
the total payment is still going for interest.

NUMBER OF PAYMENTS II: LOAN

How long will it take to pay something off with a known monthly payment? This is not an unusual question in today's finances. To calculate the number of payments, use the following equation:

$$N = \frac{\log(1 - \frac{I \cdot A}{P})}{\log(1 + I)}$$

Number of Payments Program

```
5 'NO. OF PAYMENTS
10 CLS
20 INPUT "ENTER AMOUNT OF MONTHLY
   DEPOSIT";A
30 INPUT "ENTER INTEREST RATE";I:I
   =I/1200
40 INPUT "ENTER FINAL AMOUNT";V
50 N=(LOG(V*I/A+1+I)/(LOG(1+I))-1)
60 PRINT"$"V"WILL REQUIRE DEPOSITS
   OF $"A"FOR"N"MONTHS"
```

Number of Payments Examples

If I can afford a monthly payment of $150 and the prevailing interest rate is about 12 percent, how many payments will it take to pay off a loan of $5000?

```
ENTER AMOUNT TO BE FINANCED
? 5000
ENTER INTEREST RATE IN PERCENT
? 12
ENTER AMOUNT OF AFFORDABLE MONTHLY PAYMENT
? 150
40.7 MONTHLY PAYMENTS
```

LOAN AMOUNT

Conversely, instead of how many months it will take to pay something off, let's try: "How much can I afford to spend if I commit so much per month to another payment?" The equation for this program is:

$$P = A \cdot \left(\frac{1 - (1+I)^{-N}}{I} \right)$$

Loan Amount Programs

```
5  'LOAN AMOUNT
10 CLS
20 INPUT"ENTER NUMBER OF PAYMENTS
   DESIRED";N
30 INPUT "ENTER INTEREST RATE IN P
   ERCENT";I:I=I/1200
40 INPUT "ENTER AMOUNT MONTHLY PAY
   MENT";A
50 P=A*(1-(1+I)↑-N)/I
60 PRINT"YOU CAN AFFORD TO BORROW
   $"P
```

Sample Loan Amount Programs

If I can afford to pay $100 per month for the next 15 months, how much new furniture can I purchase if the interest rate is 12 percent?

ENTER NUMBER OF PAYMENTS DESIRED
? 15
ENTER INTEREST RATE IN PERCENT
? 12
ENTER AMOUNT OF MONTHLY PAYMENT
? 100
YOU CAN AFFORD TO BORROW $ 1386.49

Current car loans have an interest rate of 10.75 percent. If a new car loan runs for 4 years, how much can I afford if my monthly payment is $ 150?

ENTER NUMBER OF PAYMENTS DESIRED
? 48
ENTER INTEREST RATE IN PERCENT
? 10.75
ENTER AMOUNT OF MONTHLY PAYMENT
? 150
YOU CAN AFFORD TO BORROW $5831.05

SINKING FUND

The last program in this chapter is for a sinking fund type of payment. The sinking fund method of payment is based on accumulating money through periodic deposits which also earn some interest. To calculate the monthly deposit use the formula:

$$A = \frac{P \cdot I}{(1+I)^N - 1}$$

Sinking Fund Program

```
5 'SINKING FUND
10 CLS
20 INPUT "ENTER AMOUNT TO BE ACCUM
   ULATED";P
30 INPUT "ENTER INTEREST RATE IN P
   ERCENT";I:I=I/100
40 INPUT "ENTER NUMBER OF YEARS OF
   ACCUMULATION";N
50 A=P*I/(((1+I)↑N)-1)
60 PRINT"YEARLY DEPOSIT IS $"INT(
   A*100+.5)/100
```

Sinking Fund Examples

How much money must be deposited at the end of each year in a 5-year sinking fund to accumulate $5000 if the annual interest rate is 7.5 percent?

ENTER AMOUNT TO BE ACCUMULATED
? 5000
ENTER INTEREST RATE IN PERCENT
? 7.5
ENTER NUMBER OF YEARS OF ACCUMULATION
? 5
YEARLY DEPOSIT IS $ 860.82

Chapter 3
Statistics

This chapter on statistics will deal with several different areas, not just the common mean standard deviation. Included are programs on curve fitting, probability, and number evaluation. Some of the problems will find use within other even larger problems. And, as mentioned in Chapter 2, some of the programs can be used to supply data for other areas.

PERMUTATIONS

The first program in this chapter deals with the operation known as permutations. Or, how many different *ordered* groups can be obtained from some set of objects without repetition. As an example, how many 3-letter permutation groups are there in the letters W, X, Y, and Z?

To solve the permutation problem requires the use of the factorial operation. To explain, 3 factorial, represented as 3!, is the product of the form 3•2•1 = 6. The 3 denotes the highest integer in the series. On the other hand, 5! would equal 120 (5•4•3•2•1 = 120).

The general equation for a permutation is:

$$M^PN = \frac{M!}{(M-N)!}$$

Therefore, the previous question of how many 3-letter permutation groups are there in the letters W, X, Y, and Z could be expressed as 4^P3.
Evaluating this expression produces $4^P3 = \dfrac{4!}{(4-3)!} = \dfrac{4!}{1!} =$

$$\frac{4 \cdot 3 \cdot 2 \cdot 1}{1} = 24.$$

Permutation Program

```
 5 'PERMUTATIONS
10 CLS
20 PRINT"INPUT M":INPUT M
30 PRINT"INPUT N":INPUT N
40 IF N=0 P=1:GOTO 110
50 IF N=1 P=N:GOTO 110
55 IF M-N<2 THEN N=M
60 FOR I=2 TO N-1
65 R(I)=M-I+1
70 IF Q=1 GOTO 80   ELSE P=M*R(I)
75 Q=1:GOTO 90
80 P=P*R(I)
90 NEXT I
100 P=P*(M-N+1)
110 PRINTM;"P";N"="P
```

Sample Permutation Problems

Evaluate 7^P5

INPUT M
? 7
INPUT N
? 5
7 P 5 = 2520

Evaluate 3^P2

INPUT M
? 3
INPUT N
? 2
3 P 3 = 6

In this example you should notice that the program has changed the problem from 3^P2 to 3^P3. This is a special case and the program changes N from 2 to 3. To check the answer

$$\frac{-3!}{1!} = \frac{3 \cdot 2 \cdot 1}{1} = 6.$$

COMBINATIONS

The difference between combinations and permutations is that a combination is *without* regard to order. For example, in the group of letters X, Y, and Z, there are 6 permutations (XY, YX, XZ, ZX, YZ, ZY). With XY and YX there is only 1 combination, XY. So, for the letters X, Y, and Z, there are 3 combinations, XY, XZ, and YZ.

The equation for combinations is:

$$M^CN = \frac{M!}{(M-N)! \cdot N!}$$

Combination Program

```
5  'COMBINATIONS
10 CLS
20 PRINT"INPUT M":INPUT M
30 PRINT"INPUT N":INPUT N
35 IF M-N<N THEN N=M-N
40 IF N=0 C=1:GOTO130
50 IF N=1 C=M:GOTO130
60 R(1)=M-N+1
70 FOR I=2 TO N-1
80 R(I)=(M-N+I)/I
90 IF Q=1 GOTO 100ELSE C=R(1)*R(I)
95 Q=1:GOTO 110
100 C=C*R(I)
110 NEXT I
120 C=C*(M/N)
130 PRINTM;;"C";N"="C
```

Sample Combination Problems

In how many ways can a group of 3 people be chosen from a larger group of 10 people? (10^c3)

```
INPUT M
? 10
INPUT N
? 3
10 C 3 = 120
```

There are 120 different ways to choose the 3 people for the smaller group.

A box contains 4 cards numbered 1 through 4. If 3 cards are drawn from the box, how many different combinations of numbers are possible?

```
INPUT M
? 4
INPUT N
? 3
4 C 3 = 4
```

ARITHMETIC MEAN

The arithmetic mean or common average of a set of numbers is the sum of those numbers divided by the quantity of numbers. For example, in the arithmetic mean, you would be asked to determine the mean of 2, 4, 3.1, 5, 6.7, 9, a total of 6 different numbers. The mean is the sum of these numbers divided by 6. Or, more specifically,

$$M = \frac{1}{n} \sum_{i=1}^{n} a_i$$

where the numbers are represented as $a_1, a_2, a_3, \ldots a_n$.

Arithmetic Mean Program

```
 5 'ARITHMETIC MEAN
10 CLS
20 PRINT"ENTER NUMBERS FOR THE ARI
   THMETIC MEAN"
30 INPUT N$
40 IF N$="/" GOTO 90
50 N=VAL(N$)
60 A=A+N
70 X=X+1
80 GOTO 30
90 PRINT"THE ARITHMETIC MEAN IS"A/
   X
```

Sample Arithmetic Mean Problems

Determine the mean of 2, 4,3. 3.1, 5, 6.7, 9 (note that in the use of this program a / is used to denote the end of the information).

ENTER NUMBERS FOR THE ARITHMETIC MEAN

? 2
? 4
? 3.1
? 5
? 6.7
? 9
? /

THE ARITHMETIC MEAN IS 4.9667

Population figures list the following as the number of children from the different families in a small rural town, 2, 4, 1, 5, 3, 10, 0, 6. What is the arithmetic mean for these families?

ENTER NUMBERS FOR THE ARITHMETIC MEAN

? 2
? 4
? 1
? 5
? 3
? 10
? 0
? 6
? /

THE ARITHMETIC MEAN IS 3.875

You'll note that even through the seventh family did not have any children, they were counted in the total number of families (8).

GEOMETRIC MEAN

The geometric mean is another type of average based on determining a specific root of a set of numbers. Using the same set of numbers 2, 4, 3.1, 5, 6.7, 9, the geometric mean is determined from the sixth root of the product of the numbers. More specifically,

$$A = \sqrt[n]{n_1 \cdot n_2 \cdot n_3 \ldots n_n}$$

Geometric Mean Program

```
5 'GEOMETRIC MEAN
10 CLS
20 PRINT"eNTER NUMBERS FOR THE GEO
   METRIC MEAN"
25 A=1
30 INPUT N$
40 IF N$=OPEN/" GOTO 90
50 N=VAL(N$)
60 A=A*N
70 X=X+1
80 GOTO 30
90 PRINT"THE GEOMETRIc MEAN IS"A^(
   1/X)
```

Geometric Mean Sample Problems

Determine the geometric mean of the examples given in the Arithmetic Mean section — 2, 4, 3.1, 5, 6.7, 9 and 2, 4, 1, 5, 3, 10, 0, 6.

ENTER NUMBERS FOR THE GEOMETRIC MEAN
? 2
? 4
? 3.1
? 5
? 6.7
? 9
? /

THE GEOMETRIC MEAN IS 4.42205

Note the difference between the arithmetic and geometric means — 4.9667 vs. 4.42205.

ENTER NUMBERS FOR THE GEOMETRIC MEAN
? 2
? 4
? 1
? 5
? 3
? 10
? 0
? 6
?/

THE GEOMETRIC MEAN IS Ø .

This example was selected to illustrate that when trying to determine a geometric mean you must have some amount for each data sample. In other words, zero is not valid data. Referring back to the equation that solves for the geometric means, we see that a zero forces a zero product. Deleting the zero produces:

ENTER NUMBERS FOR THE GEOMETRIC MEAN
? 2
? 4
? 1
? 5
? 3
? 10
? 6
? /

THE GEOMETRIC MEAN IS 3.5567
The arithmetic mean would be 4.41857.

62

HARMONIC MEAN

The last type of mean to be illustrated is the harmonic mean. Instead of being based on either a sum or product as in the arithmetic and geometric mean, the harmonic mean uses the reciprocals of the numbers in the data set. The formula for the harmonic mean is:

$$M = \frac{n}{\displaystyle\sum_{i=1}^{n} \frac{1}{ai}}$$

(where numbers are $a_1, a_2, a_3 \ldots a_n$)

Harmonic Mean Program

```
5 'HARMONIC MEAN
10 CLS
20 PRINT"ENTER NUMBERS FOR THE HAR
   MONIC MEAN"
30 INPUT N$
40 IF N$="/" GOTO 90
50 N=VAL(n$)
60 A=A+(1/N)
70 X=X+1
80 GOTO 30
90 PRINT"THE HARMONIC MEAN IS"1/(A
   /X)
```

Sample Harmonic Mean Programs

Using the numbers from the examples in the geometric mean section, determine the harmonic mean.

ENTER NUMBERS FOR THE HARMONIC MEAN

? 2
? 4
? 3.1
? 5
? 6.7
? 9
? /

THE HARMONIC MEAN IS 3.91403
ENTER NUMBERS FOR THE HARMONIC MEAN

? 2
? 4
? 1
? 5
? 3
? 10
? 6
? /

THE HARMONIC MEAN IS 2.7451

You'll again note that since reciprocals are being used, zero is invalid data since it would force a division by zero.

For the original set of data, 2, 4, 3.1, 5, 6.7, and 9, the means are:

arithmetic — 4.96670
geometric — 4.42205
harmonic — 3.91403

GROUPED DATA MEAN

There is one other type of mean that will find use in other programs, the mean of grouped data. Instead of finding the mean of fifty individual numbers, the numbers are grouped into specific categories. For example:

category	number
10-19	14
20-29	14
30-39	22
	50

Mechanically, the mean of this grouped data is found by determining the midpoint of each group, multiplying this midpoint by the number in that group to produce a category product, summing the category products, and finally dividing this sum by the total number:

category	number	midpoint	category product
10-19	14	14.5	203
20-29	14	24.5	343
30-39	22	34.5	759
	50		1305

The mean of this grouped data is 1305/50 = 26.1. The actual formula is:

$$\text{Mean} = \frac{\Sigma \, mc}{n}$$

where n is the number of pieces of data and mc is the category product.

Mean Grouped Data Program

```
5 'MEAN GROUPED
10 CLS
20 PRINT"ENTER THE RANGE OF THE PA
   RTICULAR CLASS (HIGHEST,LOWEST)
   "
25 INPUT N$(2),N$(1)-
30 IF N$(2)="/" GOTO100
40 PRINT"ENTER THE NUMBER WITHIH T
   HIS CLASS"
45 INPUT N$(3)
```

```
50 N1=VAL(N$(1)):N2=VAL(N$(2)):N3=
   VAL(N$(3))
60 M=((N2-N1)/2)+N1
70 A=(N3*M)+A
80 NT=NT+N3
90 GOTO 20
100 PRINT"THE MEAN IS"A/NT
```

Grouped Data Examples

The time between repairs of various city buses is:

time	number of buses
0-7	34
8-14	12
15-21	56
22-28	7

Find the mean time between repairs (to indicate the end of data, enter /,/ for the range).

ENTER THE RANGE OF THE PARTICULAR CLASS (HIGHEST, LOWEST)

? 7,0

ENTER THE NUMBER WITHIN THIS CLASS

? 34

ENTER THE RANGE OF THE PARTICULAR CLASS (HIGHEST, LOWEST)

? 14,8

ENTER THE NUMBER WITHIN THIS CLASS

? 12

ENTER THE RANGE OF THE PARTICULAR CLASS (HIGHEST, LOWEST)

? 21,15

ENTER THE NUMBER WITHIN THIS CLASS

? 56

ENTER THE RANGE OF THE PARTICULAR CLASS (HIGHEST, LOWEST)

? 28,22

ENTER THE NUMBER WITHIN THIS CLASS

? 7

ENTER THE RANGE OF THE PARTICULAR CLASS (HIGHEST, LOWEST)

? /,/

THE MEAN IS 13.156

Therefore, for the 109 buses in the city, each bus averaged 13.156 days between needed repairs.

Another example is one that is often seen in evaluations. Students in an Introduction to Drama course were asked to grade their instructor on a scale of 1 to 5 as to the value they received from that course, with 1 indicating little or no value and 5 indicating tremendous value. The evaluations produced the following information:

```
     Score  —  1 2 3 4 5
     Number — 15 8 9 3 21
```

What is the mean rating on this course?

Since the scores represent the actual midpoints of five infinitely small categories, the range information can be arbitrarily entered as plus or minus 1 from the midpoint. In other words, for the score 1, enter 2.0.

ENTER THE RANGE OF THE PARTICULAR CLASS (HIGHEST, LOWEST)
? 2,0
ENTER THE NUMBER WITHIN THIS CLASS
? 15
ENTER THE RANGE OF THE PARTICULAR CLASS (HIGHEST, LOWEST)
? 3,1
ENTER THE NUMBER WITHIN THIS CLASS
? 8
ENTER THE RANGE OF THE PARTICULAR CLASS (HIGHEST, LOWEST)
? 4,2
ENTER THE NUMBER WITHIN THIS CLASS
? 9
ENTER THE RANGE OF THE PARTICULAR CLASS (HIGHEST, LOWEST)
? 5,3
ENTER THE NUMBER WITHIN THIS CLASS
? 3
ENTER THE RANGE OF THE PARTICULAR CLASS (HIGHEST, LOWEST)
? 6,4
ENTER THE NUMBER WITHIN THIS CLASS
? 21
ENTER THE RANGE OF THE PARTICULAR CLASS (HIGHEST, LOWEST)
? /,/
THE MEAN IS 3.125

STANDARD DEVIATION (UNGROUPED DATA)

The various types of means have been used to determine the center of specific groups of data. The next most commonly requested piece of information is the amount of variability or the spread of the data. This standard deviation is based on the amount of variance from the mean of the data. Standard deviation is measured in the same units as the scores, whereas variance, the basis for standard deviation, is measured in the scores squared, i.e., s^2 is the symbol for variance and s is the symbol for standard deviation. The recognized formula for standard deviation is:

$$S = \sqrt{\frac{\Sigma(\overline{x} - \overline{x})^2}{n-1}}$$

Standard Deviation Program

```
5 'STANDARD DEV
10 CLS
20 PRINT"ENTER NUMBERS FOR THE STA
   NDARD DEVIATION (UNGROUPED DATA
   )"
30 INPUT N$
40 IF N$="/" GOTO 100
50 N=VAL(N$)
60 A=A+N
70 X=N[2+X
80 Y=Y+1
90 GOTO 30
100 PRINT"THE STANDARD DEVIATION I
    S"SQR((X-A*2/Y)/(Y-1))
```

Sample Standard Deviation Problems

Find the standard deviation for the data 2, 4, 3.1, 5, 6.7, 9.
ENTER NUMBERS FOR THE STANDARD DEVIATION (UN-GROUPED DATA)
? 2
? 4
? 3.1
? 5
? 6.7
? 9
? /
THE STANDARD DEVIATION IS 2.54925

Find the standard deviation for the data 2, 4, 1, 5, 3, 10, 0, 6.
ENTER NUMBERS FOR THE STANDARD DEVIATION (UN-GROUPED DATA)
? 2
? 4
? 1
? 5
? 3
? 10
? 0
? 6
? /
THE STANDARD DEVIATION IS 3.18198

STANDARD DEVIATION (GROUPED DATA)

Standard deviation for grouped data is determined in much the same way as the mean of grouped data and standard deviation. To explain, as in the mean of grouped data, a midpoint of each class is determined and then used in the standard deviation formula. This formula is:

$$S = \sqrt{\frac{\Sigma f\,(\overline{x} - \overline{x})^2}{n-1}}$$

Standard Deviation (Grouped Data) Program

```
5 'STANDARD DEV. GROUPED
10 CLS
20 PRINT"ENTER THE RANGE OF THE PA
   RTICULAR CLASS (HIGHEST,LOWEST)
   "
25 INPUT N$(2),N$(1)
30 IF N$(2)="/# IF110
40 PRINT"ENTGR THE NUMBER WITHIN T
   HIS CLASS"
45 INPUT N$(3)
50 N1=VAL(N$(1)):N2=VAL(N$(2))
   N3=VAL(N$(3))
60 M=((N2-N1)/2)+N1
70 A=(N3*M)+A
80 B=(N3*M*M)+B
90 NT=NT+N3
100 GOTO 20
110 PRINT"THE STANDARD DEVIATION I
    S"LOG((B-A♦2/NT)/(NT-1))
```

Sample Problems for Standard Deviation (Grouped Data)

Again, the time between repairs of various city buses is:

time	number of buses
0-7	34
8-14	12
15-21	56
22-28	7

Determine the standard deviation.

ENTER THE RANGE OF THE PARTICULAR CLASS (HIGHEST, LOWEST)
? 7,0
ENTER THE NUMBER WITHIN THIS CLASS
? 34
ENTER THE RANGE OF THE PARTICULAR CLASS (HIGHEST, LOWEST)
? 14,8
ENTER THE NUMBER WITHIN THIS CLASS
? 12
ENTER THE RANGE OF THE PARTICULAR CLASS (HIGHEST, LOWEST)
? 21,15
ENTER THE NUMBER WITHIN THIS CLASS
? 56
ENTER THE RANGE OF THE PARTICULAR CLASS (HIGHEST, LOWEST)
? 28,22
ENTER THE NUMBER WITHIN THIS CLASS
? 7
ENTER THE RANGE OF THE PARTICULAR CLASS (HIGHEST, LOWEST)
? /,/
THE STANDARD DEVIATION IS 7.1504

LINEAR REGRESSION

The next three programs deal with the investigation of the relationship between two variables. Considering the two variables X and Y, what mathematical formula best describes the relationship between the given points? This first program will deal with linear regression, or a set of data points or a curve that approximates a straight line. The general equation for a straight line is $Y = MX + B$. From the data points it will be necessary to solve for the constants M and B which give the closest agreement. In addition to providing the constants, the program also solves for the coefficient of determination, a measure that indicates how closely the equation fits the initial data. The coefficient of determination is between 0 and 1, and the closer it is to 1 the better the equation fits.

Solving for the constants uses a method of least squares. The equations are:

$$S = \frac{\Sigma_{xy} - \frac{\Sigma_x \Sigma_y}{n}}{\Sigma x^2 - \frac{(\Sigma_x)^2}{n}}$$

$$T = \overline{y} - S\,\overline{X}$$

$$\text{where } \overline{y} = \frac{\Sigma y}{n}$$

$$\overline{x} = \frac{\Sigma_x}{n}$$

$$R = \frac{\left(\Sigma_{xy} - \frac{\Sigma_x \Sigma_y}{n}^2\right)}{\left(\Sigma_x^2 - \frac{(\Sigma_x)^2}{n}\right)\left(\Sigma_y^2 - \frac{(\Sigma_y)^2}{n}\right)}$$

Linear Regression Program

```
5 'LINEAR REGRESSION
10 CLS
20 PRINT"ENTER THE GROUPS OF DATA
   POINTS (X,Y)
```

```
30  INPUT N$(1),N$(2)
40  IF N$(1)="/" GOTO 110
50  N1=VAL(N$(1)):N2=VAL(N$(2))
60  A=N1*N2+A
70  XT=N1+XT
80  YT=N2+YT
90  XS=N1*N1+XS
95  YS=N2*N2+YS
100 X=X+1
105 GOTO 30
110 S=(A-(XT*YT/X))/(XS-((XT↑2)/X)
    )
120 T=YT/X-(S*(XT/X))
130 R=(X*A-(XT*YT))/(SQR(X*XS-(XT↑
    2))*(SQR(X*YS-(YT↑2))))
140 PRINT"FOR THE GENERAL EQUATION
     Y=MX+B, M="S"AND B="T"."CHR$(
    13)"THE COEFFICIENT OF DETERMI
    NATION IS"R↑2
```

Sample Linear Regression Problems

You want to use a thermometer to measure the outside temperature at the top of a mountain. Unfortunately, the only thermometer that you can buy locally is measured in Centigrade. However, you do have an inside thermometer which is marked in Fahrenheit, but it only goes down to freezing, 32 degrees. How do you measure the outside temperature?

One method might be to immerse both thermometers in a bowl of very hot water and record the temperatures of both thermometers as the water cools. From this information, you could determine the exact relationship between the two thermometers and calculate the outside temperature in Fahrenheit.

The readings as the water cools are:

Fahrenheit	Centigrade
180	82
142	61
133	56
105	40
90	32
73	23
64	18
50	10

ENTER THE GROUPS OF DATA POINTS (X,Y)
? 82,180
? 61,142
? 56,133
? 40,105
? 32,90
? 23,73
? 18,64
? 10,50
? /,/
FOR THE GENERAL EQUATION Y=MX+B, M=1 1.80864 AND B= 31.8274.
THE COEFFICIENT OF DETERMINATION IS .999922

This example was selected since the conversion equation between Centigrade and Fahrenheit is well known (F = 1.8C + 32) and readily fits the general equation for a straight line. Linear regression can be used in many ways to help correlate/extrapolate data. Consider Fig. 3-1 and find the equation that best describes the data.

ENTER THE GROUPS OF DATA POINTS (X,Y)
? 1.25,1.1
? 3,3.4
? 4.5,5.2
? 6,7.2
? /,/
FOR THE GENERAL EQUATION Y=MX+B, M= 1.27648 AND
B=−.482017
THE COEFFICIENT OF DETERMINATION IS .999636

So, from the four selected data points, the general equation of a line that best describes the data has been determined. From this line and equation, the data can be extrapolated out through values of 12 for X.

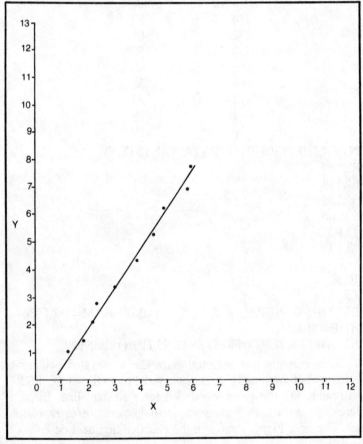

Fig. 3-1. To be used in solving a linear regression problem.

X	Y
1	.79
2	2.07
3	3.35
8	9.73
9	11.01
10	12.28
11	13.56
12	14.84

LOGRITHMIC CURVE FIT

This next program is very similar to linear regression, except that, instead of being a straight-line type of relationship, it is a function of the natural log (e) of X. Fitting to a logrithmic curve uses the general equation $Y = M1nX + B$. The logrithmic curve is a typical form in that one axis of the curve is compressed in relation to the other. The following examples will clearly show this relationship. The equations used to solve for the logrithmic curve fit are:

$$S = \frac{\Sigma y \ln x - \dfrac{1}{n}(\Sigma \ln x \Sigma y)}{\Sigma (\ln x)^2 - \dfrac{1}{n}(\Sigma \ln x)^2}$$

$$T = \frac{1}{n}(\Sigma y - S\Sigma \ln x)$$

$$R = \frac{(\Sigma y \, \ln x - \dfrac{1}{n}(\Sigma \ln x \Sigma \ln y))^2}{(\Sigma(\ln x)^2 - \dfrac{1}{n}(\Sigma \ln x)^2)(\Sigma y^2 - \dfrac{1}{n}(\Sigma y)^2)}$$

Logrithmic Curve Fit Program

```
5 'LOG CURVE FIT
10 CLS
20 PRINT"ENTER THE GROUPS OF DATA
   POINTS (X,Y)
30 INPUT N$(1),N$(2)
40 IF N$(1)="/" GOTO 130
50 N1=VAL(N$(1)):N2=VAL(N$(2))
60 A=A+N2*LOG(N1)
70 B=B+LOG(N1)
75 I=I+N2
80 C=C+(LOG(N1))^2
85 F=F+N2^2
90 G=G+LOG(N1)
100 D=B^2
```

```
110  X=X+1
120  GOTO 30
130  E=(A-B*I/X)/(C-D/X)
140  H=(I-E*G)/X
150  PRINT"iN THE GENERAL FORM OF Y
     =M(LN(X))+B, M="E"AND X="H"."
160  J=((A-B*I/X)*2)/((C-D/X)*(F-((
     I*2)/X)))
165  PRINT"THE COEFFICIENT OF DETER
     MINATION IS"J
```

Sample Logrithmic Curve Fit Problems

Determine the equation of the line shown in Fig. 3-1. As can be seen, the curve can not be stretched to produce a straight line and the data points seem to compress as the values for X get bigger. Therefore, this is a good candidate for logrithmic curve fit program. Four data points were selected.

X	Y
2	.5
4	1.5
6.3	2.25
9.5	2.75

If the coefficient of determination is not high enough, additional points can be selected and the program run again.
ENTER THE GROUPS OF DATA POINTS (X,Y)
? 2,.5
? 4,1.5
? 6.3,2.25
? 9.5,2.75
? /,/
IN THE GENERAL FORM OF $Y+M(LN(X))+B$, M= 1.46487 AND B=−.510028.
THE COEFFICIENT OF DETERMINATION IS .997925.

Again, with four point, you have been able to determine the equation of the line that produces the best fit through the data points. More points could have been added, though it is a matter of diminishing returns as to whether the additional time is worthwhile for the small increase in accuracy. For example, adding the additional points 1.45,0 and 7.5,2.5 changes M to 1.48962, X to −.541302, and raises the coefficient of determination to .998624, a very small change in accuracy rating. The actual equation of the line for this example was $Y = 1.51nX − 0.5$.

EXPONENTIAL CURVE FIT

The last curve fit program is for data that exhibits an exponential type of progression. You'll notice that the curve in Fig. 3-3 is somewhat similar to that of Fig. 3-2 in that it seems to approach some limit. This is a case where it might be easiest to run the data set in both the exponential and logrithmic curve programs to determine the best fit. However, in some cases, inferences can be made because of the data range to help select the appropriate program to use.

The equations to solve the exponential curve fit problem are:

$$S = \frac{\Sigma x \ln y - \dfrac{1}{n} (\Sigma x)(\Sigma/ny)}{\Sigma x^2 - \dfrac{1}{n} (\Sigma x)^2}$$

$$T = EXP \left(\frac{\Sigma \ln y}{n} - S \frac{\Sigma x}{n} \right)$$

$$R = \frac{(\Sigma x \ln y - \dfrac{1}{n}(\Sigma x \Sigma \ln Y))^2}{\left(\Sigma x^2 - \dfrac{(\Sigma x)^2}{n} \right) \left(\Sigma (\ln Y)^2 - \dfrac{(\Sigma \ln Y)^2}{n} \right)}$$

Exponential Curve Fit Program

```
5  'EXP. CURVE FIT
10 CLS
20 PRINT"ENTER THE GROUPS OF DATA
   POINTS (X,Y)
30 INPUT N$(1),N$(2)
40 IF N$(1)="/" GOTO 130
50 N1=VAL(N$(1)):N2=VAL(N$(2))
60 A=A+N1*LOG(N2)
70 B=B+LOG(N2)
75 I=I+N1
80 C=C+N1^2
85 D=D+N1
90 F=D[ 2
```

81

```
100 G=G+(LOG(N2)↑2)
110 X=X+1
120 GOTO 30
130 E=(A-B*I/X)/(C-F/X)
140 H=EXP(B/X-E*I/X)
150 PRINT"iN THE GENERAL FORM OF Y
    =M*E[BX, M="E"AND X="H"."
160 J=((A-B*I/X)↑2)/((C-F/X)*(G-((
    B[2)/X)))
165 PRINT"THE COEFFICIENT OF DETER
    MINATION IS"J
```

Sample Exponential Curve Fit Problem

Using Fig. 3-3, solve for the equation that best describes the line in the data points.

X	Y
1	.9
3	.35
5	.13
7	.04

ENTER THE GROUPS OF DATA POINTS (X,Y)
? 1,.9
? 3,.35
? 5,.13
? 7,.04
? /,/
IN THE GENERAL FORM OF Y=M*E!BX, B=−.516547 AND M=1.58822.
THE COEFFICIENT OF DETERMINATION IS .997247.

Running the same data set in the logrithmic curve fit program produces: B= .881006 and M=−.452093 and a coefficient of determination of .991973. Since the two coefficients of determination are so close, it might be wise to use additional points to find the best fit. However, using more data points is not without its problems. Since there are more points, the amount of error tends to reduce the coefficients of determination.

For example, consider the following data set:

X	Y
1	.9
3	.35
5	.13
7	.04
2	.51
6	.75
10	.015

When applied to the exponential curve fit program, B now equals −.421978, M = 1.48592, and the coefficient of determination is .71439. You'll notice that even though the changes in B and M are relatively small, the coefficient of determination has decreased significantly. With the increased number of data points, any error is now more significant. For comparison, when using the logrithmic curve fit program, B = .32053, M = .817324, and the coefficient of

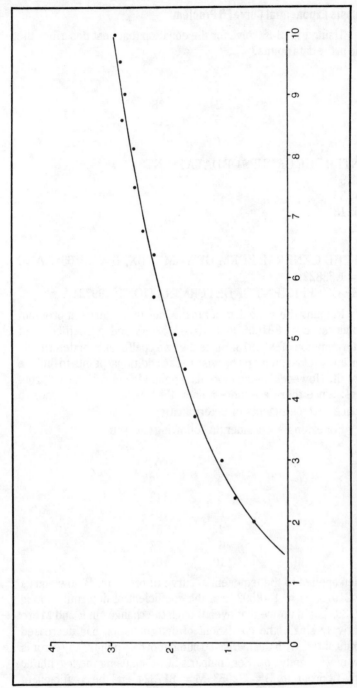

Fig. 3-2. To be used in solving a logrithmic curve fit problem.

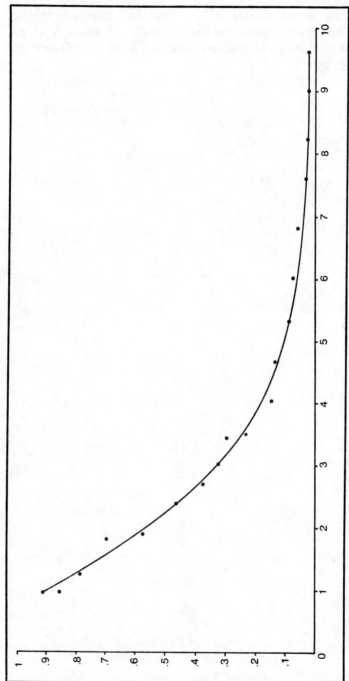

Fig. 3-3. To be used in solving an exponential curve fit problem.

determination is .536147. So, increasing the number of data points has lowered the confidence levels overall for B and M, yet they have provided greater assurance that the correct curve fit program is being used.

FACTORIAL

As mentioned earlier in this chapter, a factorial, N, is the simple progression N • (N−1) • (N−2) . . . (2) • (1). Integers must be used.

Factorial Program

```
5 'FACTORIAL
10 CLS
20 INPUT"ENTER AN INTEGER";N
30 M=1
40 FOR I=1 TO N
50 M=M*I
60 NEXT I
70 PRINT"THE FACTORIAL OF"N"IS"M
```

Sample Factorial Problems

ENTER AN INTEGER
? 9
THE FACTORIAL OF 9 IS 362880
ENTER AN INTEGER
? 24
THE FACTORIAL OF 24 IS 6.20448E+23

CHI-SQUARE EVALUATION

The last program in this chapter deals with chi-square tests or evaluations. This evaluation can be used to determine two pieces of information: "goodness of fit," and where two variables are related or independent. Since this is not a book devoted to statistics, but one that shows how many different types of programs can be computerized for everyday use, I am not going to explain the complete procedure for using the chi-square evaluation. However, this program will solve for chi-square, which can then be used to determine goodness of fit and any relationship between variables.

The chi-square evaluation calculates the relationship between the observed frequency and the expected frequency in the distribution of samples. The formula is:

$$X^2 \sum \frac{(O_i - E_i)^2}{E_i}$$

Chi-Square Evaluation Program

```
5  'CHI-SQUARE EVAL.
10 CLS
20 PRINT"ENTER THE OBSERVED FREQUE
   NCY,EXPECTED FREQUENCY INFORMAT
   ION"
25 INPUT O$,E$
30 IF O$="/" GOTO70
40 O=VAL(O$):E=VAL(E$)
50 KI=KI+((O-E)^2)/E
60 GOTO 25
70 PRINT"THE CHI-SQUARE EVALUATION
    IS"KI
```

Chi-Square Sample Problems

Determine Chi-Square for the following information.

Observed	Expected
20	30
60	90
110	120
50	30
60	30

ENTER THE OBSERVED FREQUENCY, EXPECTED FRE-
QUENCY INFORMATION

? 20,30

? 60,90

? 110,120

? 50,30

? 60,30

? /,/

THE CHI-SQUARE EVALUATION IS 57.5

As I said, this information will now be used to determine
whether the assumed hypothesis is true or false.

Chapter 4
Electronics Programs

This next chapter is devoted to programs encountered in many facets of electrical engineering. Admittedly, there are an infinite number of equations used in the field of electrical engineering, but these programs represent a fair cross section. There are also programs which might not ordinarily be at one's fingertips for instant use. In this chapter I will start going into detailed explanations of the programs themselves. So far in this book, the programs have generally not been sufficiently complicated to warrant a closer examination. However, in this chapter, a number of programs contain smaller programs which can be used either singly or in combinations to solve other problems.

ANTENNA PATTERN

This first program of the chapter will be used to determine the radiation pattern of vertical antennas. In many cases, the radiation pattern can be found by checking any of the many reference texts available which show patterns for "common" antenna configurations. The problem arises when certain factors dictate antenna positioning that does not fall into a common configuration. At such a time this program proves invaluable.

To compute the radiation pattern from a group of vertical radiators requires that you know the antenna spacing, phase difference, individual antenna currents, and positional location between the antennas. Figure 4-1 shows a diagram that will be used to explain the designations used in the program. In this diagram there are three antennas, with one designated as the reference antenna. The other two are located both in spacing and distance from this reference antenna. In addition to the physical positions, the second two antennas are related to the reference by their individual antenna currents and phase. The four designators for the antennas are:

Antenna Current	C
Phase relationship to the reference	P
Spacing from the reference	S
Angular Displacement from the reference	AD

The last quantity, angular displacement, is used to orient the pattern in either a relative or true plane. To explain, if you are only concerned with the pattern relative to the antennas, use zero as the angular displacement for Antenna 1 and 60 degrees as the angular displacement for Antenna 2 (see Fig. 4-1). If you want to determine the pattern base on True North, use the actual true bearing from the reference to the selected antenna. Lines 50 through 150 of the Antenna Pattern program are used to input this data. The first input statement, line 20, sets the number of points at which the data will be plotted. In effect, it determines the number of times the pattern information will be summed. Line 50 inputs the total number of verticals in the antenna system. Note that this value, E, is decreased by 1 to take into account the reference element. The complete equation to determine the antenna pattern is:

$$A(\theta) = \left| \; + \sum_{n=1}^{N-1} A^1_n e j^{\psi m} \; \right|$$

Lines 160 through 270 of the program do the actual summing to determine the relative amplitude of the pattern for each plotting point. Note that in lines 200 and 210 the formula for resolving a polar form of notation to rectangular coordinates is used. The respective X and Y quantities are then summed in lines 220 and 230 each time through the loop. Once the required number of loops have been completed, as determined by the number of elements, line 260 converts the X and Y information back to a polar notation. From here, line 270 returns back to line 170 to repeat this entire process for the next plotting point.

Lines 275-430 show the display portion of the program. In this section, the information is formatted into three columns for presentation. Lines 271 through 300 display the information in a relative amplitude format. More useful than the relative amplitude format is one that presents the information after being normalized to the largest value. This program will present either normalized data or normalized data expressed in dB. Lines 310 and 320 search the information file to determine the largest value for use in the normalized data.

Antenna Pattern Program

```
5  'ANTENNA PATTERN
10 CLS
20 INPUT "ENTER NUMBER OF DEGREES
   BETWEEN PLOTTING POINTS";D
```

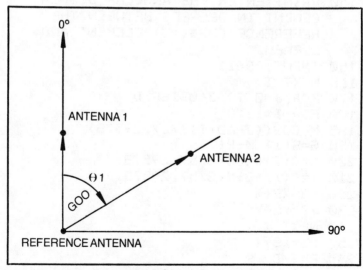

Fig. 4-1. Reference antenna with two other variably located antennas.

```
30 DIMN(360/D)
35 PRINT
45 PRINT"THE REFERENCE ELEMENT IS
   DESIGNATED AS ELEMENT 0"
49 PRINT
50 INPUT"ENTER THE TOTAL NUMBER OF
   ELEMENTS";E
55 PRINT
60 E=E-1
70 FOR I=1 TO E
80 PRINT"FOR ELEMENT"I"ENTER THE A
   NTENNA CURRENT."
90 INPUT C(I)
100 PRINT"ENTER THE PHASE DIFFEREN
    CE BETWEEN ELEMENT"I"AND THE R
    EFERENCE"CHR$(13)"ELEMENT."
101 PRINT"USE + FOR LAGGING AND -
    FOR LEADING."
110 INPUTP(I)
120 PRINT"ENTER THE SPACING IN DEG
    REES (ONE WAVELENGTH = 360 DEG
    REES)"CHR$(13)"BETWEEN ELEMENT
    "I"AND THE REFERENCE"
130 INPUTS(I)
140 PRINT"ENTER THE ANGULAR DISPLA
    CEMENT IN DEGREES BETWEEN THE
    REFERENCE"CHR$(13)"ELEMENT AND
    ELEMENT"I
150 INPUT AD(I)
160 NEXT I
170 FOR J=0 TO 360STEP D
180 FOR I=1 TO E
185 M=COS((J-AD(I))/57.29578)
190 G=S(I)*M-P(I)
200 X=C(I)*COS(G/57.29578)
210 Y=C(I)*SIN(G/57.29578)
220 XS=XS+X
230 YS=YS+Y
240 NEXT I
250 XS=XS+1
255 F=J/D
260 N(F)=SQR(XS[ 2+YS[ 2)
```

94

```
261 XS=0
262 YS=0
270 NEXT J
271 CLS
275 PRINTTAB(9)"MAG."TAB(29)"MAG."
    TAB(50)"MAG."
280 FOR Q=0 TO 110 STEP D
295 PRINTQ+DTAB(5)"DEG"TAB(8)N((Q+
    D)/D)TAB(20)Q+D+120TAB(25)"DEG
    "TAB(28)N((Q+D+120)/D)TAB(41)G
    +D+240TAB(46)"DEG"TAB(49)N((Q+
    D+240)/D)
300 NEXT Q
310 FOR R=0 TO 360/D
320 IF N(R)>NG THEN NG=N(R):NEXT R
    ELSE NEXT R
340 INPUT"DO YOU WANT NORMALIZED D
    ATA?";ND$
345 IF ND$="Y"GOTO 347
346 END
347 CLS
348 PRINTTAB(9)"MAG."TAB(29)"MAG."
    TAB(50)"MAG."
350 FOR Q=0 TO 110 STEP D
360 PRINTQ+DTAB(5)"DEG"TAB(8)N((Q+
    D)/D)/NGTAB(20)Q+D+120TAB(25)"
    DEG"TAB(28)N((Q+D+120)/D)/NGTA
    B(41)Q+D+240TAB(46)"DEG"TAB(49
    )N((Q+D+240)/D)/NG
370 NEXT Q
380 INPUT"DO YOU WANT NORMALIZED D
    ATA EXPRESSED IN DB?";DB$
390 IF DB$="Y"THENGOTO 400
395 END
400 CLS
410 PRINTTAB(9)"DB"TAB(29)"DB"TAB(
    50)"DB"
415 FOR Q=0 TO 110 STEP D
420 PRINTQ+DTAB(5)"DEG"TAB(8)20*(L
    OG(N((Q+D)/D)/NG)/LOG(10))TAB(
    21)Q+D+120TAB(27)"DEG"TAB(30)2
    0*(LOG(N((Q+D+120)/D)/NG)/LOG(
```

```
          10))TAB(43)Q+D+240TAB(47)"DEG"
          TAB(51)20*(LOG(N((Q+D+240)/D)/
          NG)/LOG(10))
      430 NEXT Q
```

Where
$A(\theta)$ = pattern amplitude as a function of θ

A_n^1 = relative amplitude of the nth element

N = total number of elements

$\psi_n = \beta d_n \cos(\theta_n - \theta) - \alpha_n$

α_n = phase of the nth element relative to the
reference element in degrees (+ for lagging,
− for leading phase)

βd_n = electrical distance (in degrees) from the
driven element to the nth element

θ_n = spatial angle between elements.

Sample Antenna Pattern Problem

For this example, use Fig. 4-1. The spacing between the Reference Antenna and Antenna 1 is 0.5 wavelengths (180 degrees) and between the Reference and Antenna 2 is 1 wavelength. Antenna 2's angular displacement is 60 degrees. The current in Antenna 1 is 1 and in Antenna 2 is 2. The phase between the reference and Antenna 1 is 90 leading and between the reference and Antenna 2 is 180 degrees leading. Determine the normalized amplitude in dB every 30 degrees.

ENTER NUMBER OF DEGREES BETWEEN PLOTTING POINTS? 45
THE REFERENCE ELEMENT IS DESIGNATED AS ELEMENT Ø
ENTER THE TOTAL NUMBER OF ELEMENTS? 3
FOR ELEMENT 1 ENTER THE ANTENNA CURRENT.
? 1
ENTER THE PHASE DIFFERENCE BETWEEN ELEMENT 1 AND THE REFERENCE ELEMENT. Use + FOR LAGGING AND − FOR LEADING.
? −90
ENTER THE SPACING IN DEGREES (ONE WAVELENGTH = 360 DEGREES) BETWEEN ELEMENT 1 AND THE REFERENCE
? 180

ENTER THE ANGULAR DISPLACEMENT IN DEGREES BE-
TWEEN THE REFERENCE ELEMENT AND ELEMENT 1
? Ø
FOR ELEMENT 2 ENTER THE ANTENNA CURRENT.
? 2
ENTER THE PHASE DIFFERENCE BETWEEN ELEMENT 2
AND THE REFERENCE ELEMENT. USE + FOR LAGGING
AND – FOR LEADING.
? –180
ENTER THE SPACING IN DEGREES (ONE WAVELENGTH =
360 DEGREES)
BETWEEN ELEMENT 2 AND THE REFERENCE
? 360
ENTER THE ANGULAR DISPLACEMENT IN DEGREES BE-
TWEEN THE REFERENCE ELEMENT AND ELEMENT 2
? 60

MAG.	MAG.	MAG.
30 DEG .940224	150 DEG 1.08759	270 DEG .593411
60 DEG 2	180 DEG 3.16228	300 DEG 2
90 DEG 2.51373	210 DEG 2.40561	330 DEG 1.67844
120 DEG 4	240 DEG 1.12352E-06	360 DEG 3.16228

DO YOU WANT NORMALIZED DATA?? Y

MAG.	MAG.	MAG.
30 DEG .235056	150 DEG .271897	270 DEG .148353
60 DEG .5	180 DEG .790569	300 DEG .5
90 DEG .628432	210 DEG .601402	330 DEG .419609
120 DEG 1	240 DEG 2.8088E-07	360 DEG .79057

DO YOU WANT NORMALIZED DATA EXPRESSED IN DB?? Y

MAG.	MAG.	MAG.
30 DEG-12.5766	150 DEG-11.3119	270 DEG-16.5741
60 DEG-6.0206	180 DEG-2.0412	300 DEG-6.0206
90 DEG-4.03484	210 DEG-4.4167	330 DEG-7.5431
120 DEG 0	240 DEG-131.03	360 DEG-2.04119

GAMMA MATCH

The next two programs are also antenna-related, being designed to provide matching information between an antenna and a transmission system. The first, the Gamma Match Program, will determine the necessary dimensions for a Gamma Match on the driven element of a Yagi antenna. However, the Yagi antenna is not the only applicable type of antenna. Vertical antennas can also be shunt fed using the same type of matching arrangement.

As with the last program on antenna patterns, this program uses many smaller operations to obtain the final answer, computing the impedance of two parallel conductors, polar to rectangular conversions, and Smith Chart operations. Again, the complete program will be explained in small sections so that you can understand the operations and use any portions for your own programs.

First, see Fig. 4-2. This diagram illustrates the gamma match and shows the designations used in the program. Each is relatively self-explanatory. Note that the spacing between the driven element and gamma rod is the spacing between the inner edges of the two pieces. Each of the spacings is entered in inches, the impedances in ohms, and the frequency in megahertz.

Lines 90 through 110 of the Gamma Match Program compute the impedance step-up ratio between the gamma rod and driven element by the following formula:

$$ r = \left(1 + \frac{\log \dfrac{2S}{d_1}^z}{\log \dfrac{2S}{d_z}} \right) $$

where S = center-to-center spacing
 d_z = diameter of driven element
 d_1^z = diameter of rod

This ratio must be computed to compensate for the unequal diameters of the element and gamma rod which act as a section of transmission line.

Since these two pieces do act as a section of transmission line that has been short circuited at one end, they will add some additional reactance that must be taken into account during the calculations. Line 120 computes the impedance of this section of transmission line. The formula for this equation is:

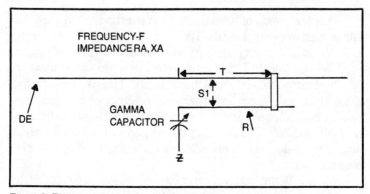

Fig. 4-2. The gamma match and designations used in the program.

$$Z_0 = 60 \cosh^{-1} \frac{45^2 - d_2^2 - d_1^2}{2\,d_2 d_1} \text{ ohms}$$

The next step is to determine the increased impedance of the driven element over its center-point impedance caused by its being fed off center (tap point of gamma rod). Line 130 does double duty by not only calculating this increased impedance, but also multiplies this product by the previously determined step-up ratio. At this point, RI and XI represent the real and imaginary components of the inital input impedance. Lines 140 and 150 calculate the impedance after the RI and XI values have been added to the reactance caused by the short-circuited section of the transmission line. These new values, RI(2) and XI(2), represent the real and imaginary components which will be rotated around the Smith Chart. The amount of rotation is determined by the length of the gamma rod vs. the frequency of operation. Lines 160, 170, and 180 perform the actual rotation calculations. The formula for this rotation is:

$$Z = \left(\frac{RI1 + j\,XI1}{RI2 + j\,XI2} \right) R_o$$

where $RI1 = R_L$
   $XI1 = R_o X_K + X_L$
   $RI2 = R_o - X_L X_K$
   $XI2 = R_i X_K$

The division performed in line 180 is a complex type of division. That is, it is performed in a polar notation by dividing the magnitudes and subtracting the phase angles.

The next group of lines starts by converting the M3 and A3 values back to the rectangular type of notation in line 190. Next, lines 210 and 220 convert the series equivalent of the impedance to a parallel equivalent. This is done so that the reactance caused by the short-circuited section of transmission line can be directly added to the parallel equivalent. Once this reactance is added, line 230, the parallel equivalent, is converted back to the series form in lines 240 and 260. And finally, the real part of the impedance is multiplied by the system impedance to produce the final real and imaginary parts.

In line 270, the final real part of the impedance is compared to the transmission system impedance. If the difference is less than 1 percent, the value of the gamma capacitor is calculated and displayed. Otherwise, the program will change the value of T, the distance to the tap point, and go through the entire series of calculations again. Initially, the change to T is one inch. However, once the difference is less than 5 ohms, but more than 1 percent, T is either incremented or decremented by 0.25 inch until a calculation shows a difference of less than 1 percent.

The final group of lines, lines 350 to the end, are used to change any of the initial parameters for recalculations.

Gamma Match Program

```
1 'GAMMA MATCH
2 CLS
3 PRINT"THIS PROGRAM IS DESIGNED TO DETERMINE THE FINAL TAP POINT"
4 PRINT"AND VALUE OF THE SERIES CAPACITOR IN A GAMMA MATCH.  THE"
5 PRINT"PROGRAM WILL TAKE THE INITIAL DATA AND GO THROUGH MULTIPLE"
6 PRINT"ITERATIONS UNTIL A SUITABLE MATCH HAS BEEN DETERMINED."
7 PRINT"THE FINAL TAP POINT WILL BE WITHIN ONE QUARTER OF AN INCH."
8 PRINT"THIS WILL PROVIDE A SUFFICIENTLY ACCURATE STARTING POINT"
9 PRINT"FOR AN ACTUAL ANTENNA.":PRINT
10 INPUT "ENTER DIAMETER OF ELEMENT";DE
20 INPUT "ENTER DIAMETER OF GAMMA ROD";DR
30 INPUT "ENTER SPACING BETWEEN ELEMENT AND ROD";S1
40 INPUT "ENTER TRANSMISSION SYSTEM IMPEDANCE";Z
50 INPUT "ENTER RESISTIVE PORTION OF ANTENNA IMPEDANCE";RA
60 INPUT "ENTER REACTIVE PORTION OF ANTENNA IMPEDANCE";XA
70 INPUT "ENTER FREQUENCY IN MEGAHERTZ";F
80 INPUT "ENTER DISTANCE IN INCHES FROM CENTER OF DRIVEN
ELEMENT TO CENTER OF GAMMA ROD SHORTING STRAP";T:T(1)=T
85 S=DE/2+DR/2+S1
90 X=((4*S*S)-(DE^2)+(DR^2))/(4*S*DR):X1=LOG(X+SQR(X*X-1))
100 Y=((4*S*S)+(DE^2)-(DR^2))/(4*S*DE):Y1=LOG(Y+SQR(Y*Y-1))
```

```
110 HZ=(1+X1/Y1)↑2
120 ZL1=((4*S*S)-(DR↑2))/(2*DE*DR):ZL=60*(LOG(ZL1+SQR(ZL1*ZL1-1
130 RI=HZ*RA/(COS(T*F*5.32343E-04))↑2:XI=HZ*XA/(COS(T*F*5.32343E-04))+XI
140 RI(1)=RI:XI(1)=(ZL*TAN(T*F*5.32343E-04))+XI
150 RI(2)=ZL-(XI*TAN(T*F*5.32343E-04)):XI(2)=RI*TAN(T*F*5.32343E-04)
160 M1=((RI(1))↑2+(XI(1))↑2)↑.5:A1=ATN(XI(1)/RI(1))*57.2958
170 M2=((RI(2))↑2+(XI(2))↑2)↑.5:A2=ATN(XI(2)/RI(2))*57.2958
180 M3=M1/M2:A3=A1-A2
190 RR=M3*COS(A3*.01745329):XR=(M3*SIN(A3*.01745329))
200 RS=RR:XS=XR
210 M4=1/((XS↑2+RS↑2)↑.5:A4=-ATN(XS/RS)*57.2958
220 RP=M4*COS(A4*.01745329):XP=M4*SIN(A4*.01745329)
230 XT=XP+(-1/TAN(T*F*5.32343E-04))
240 M5=1/((RP↑2+XT↑2)↑.5:A5=-ATN(XT/RP)*57.2958
250 RS(1)=M5*COS(A5*.01745329):XS(1)=M5*SIN(A5*.01745329)
260 RF=ZL*RS(1):XF=ZL*XS(1)
270 IF ABS(RF-Z)/Z/100 PRINT"THE FINAL RESISTANCE IS";RF"(A DIF
    FERENCE OF LESS THAN 1 PERCENT).  THE NEW TAP POINT IS AT";
    T;"INCHES.  THE GAMMA"CHR$(13)"CAPACITOR IS";1E6/(2*3.1416*
    F*XF);"PICOFARADS":GOTO 350 ELSE 272
272 PRINTT"INCHES",RF"OHMS"
280 IF RF<Z GOTO 310
290 IF ABS(RF-Z)<5 T=T-.25:GOTO 130 ELSE T=T-1:GOTO 130
310 IF ABS(RF-Z)<5 T=T+.25:GOTO 130 ELSE T=T+1:GOTO 130
```

```
350 PRINT"AGAIN?    (1=YES,  0=NO)":INPUT Q
351 IF Q=0 THEN END
352 PRINT"ENTER THE PARAMETER YOU WANT TO CHANGE"
353 PRINTTAB(10)"ELEMENT DIAMETER      1"
354 PRINTTAB(10)"ROD DIAMETER          2"
355 PRINTTAB(10)"SPACING               3"
356 PRINTTAB(10)"SYSTEM IMPEDANCE      4"
357 PRINTTAB(10)"ANTENNA RESISTANCE    5"
358 PRINTTAB(10)"ANTENNA REACTANCE     6"
359 PRINTTAB(10)"FREQUENCY             7"
361 INPUT N
362 IF N=1 PRINT"NEW ELEMENT DIAMETER?":INPUT DE
363 IF N=2 PRINT"NEW ROD DIAMETER?":INPUT DR
364 IF N=3 PRINT"NEW SPACING?":INPUT S1
365 IF N=4 PRINT"NEW SYSTEM IMPEDANCE?":INPUT Z
366 IF N=5 PRINT"NEW ANTENNA RESISTANCE?":INPUT RA
367 IF N=6 PRINT"NEW ANTENNA REACTANCE?":INPUT XA
368 IF N=7 PRINT"NEW FREQUENCY?":INPUT F
370 T=T(1):GOTO 85
```

Sample Gamma Match Program

Determine the correct tap point and gamma capacitor value for an antenna and Gamma Match system with the following characteristics:

Driven Element Diameter	1 inch
Gamma Rod Diameter	.375 inch
Inside Spacing	4 inches
Transmission System Impedance	50 ohms
Real Part of Antenna Impedance	35 ohms
Imaginary Part of Antenna Impedance	−35 ohms
Frequency	16 Megahertz
Distance to Tap Point	24 inches

(Each time the program goes through a set of calculations that does not produce a difference of less than 1 percent, the tap point distance goes back through its calculations until the right tap point is found.)

THIS PROGRAM IS DESIGNED TO DETERMINE THE FINAL TAP POINT AND VALUE OF THE SERIES CAPACITOR IN A GAMMA MATCH. THE PROGRAM WILL TAKE THE INITIAL DATA AND GO THROUGH MULTIPLE ITERATIONS UNTIL A SUITABLE MATCH HAS BEEN DETERMINED. THE FINAL TAP POINT WILL BE WITHIN ONE QUARTER OF AN INCH. THIS WILL PROVIDE A SUFFICIENTLY ACCURATE STARTING POINT FOR AN ACTUAL ANTENNA.
ENTER DIAMETER OF ELEMENT? 1
ENTER DIAMETER OF GAMMA ROD? .375
ENTER SPACING BETWEEN ELEMENT AND ROD? 4
ENTER TRANSMISSION SYSTEM IMPEDANCE? 50
ENTER RESISTIVE PORTION OF ANTENNA IMPEDANCE? 35
ENTER REACTIVE PORTION OF ANTENNA IMPEDANCE? −35
ENTER FREQUENCY IN MEGAHERTZ? 16
ENTER DISTANCE IN INCHES FROM CENTER OF DRIVEN ELEMENT TO CENTER OF GAMMA ROD SHORTING STRAP? 24

24 INCHES	21.5639 OHMS
25 INCHES	24.0441 OHMS
26 INCHES	26.7077 OHMS
27 INCHES	29.5588 OHMS

28 INCHES	32.6002 OHMS
29 INCHES	35.8341 OHMS
30 INCHES	39.2608 OHMS
31 INCHES	42.8794 OHMS
32 INCHES	46.6872 OHMS
32.25 INCHES	47.6684 OHMS
32.5 INCHES	48.6609 OHMS

THE FINAL RESISTANCE IS 49.6648 (A DIFFERENCE OF
LESS THAN 1 PERCENT). THE NEW TAP POINT IS AT 32.75
INCHES. THE GAMMA CAPACITOR IS 93.4315 PICOFARADS
AGAIN? (1=YES, 0=NO)
? 1
ENTER THE PARAMETER YOU WANT TO CHANGE

ELEMENT DIAMETER	1
ROD DIAMETER	2
SPACING	3
SYSTEM IMPEDANCE	4
ANTENNA RESISTANCE	5
ANTENNA REACTANCE	6
FREQUENCY	7

? 7
NEW FREQUENCY?
? 21
24 INCHES   44.7599 OHMS
THE FINAL RESISTANCE IS 49.9176 (A DIFFERENCE OF
LESS THAN 1 PERCENT). THE NEW TAP POINT IS 25
INCHES. THE GAMMA
CAPACITOR IS 71.0716 PICOFARADS
AGAIN? (1=YES, 0=NO)
? 0
READY

As can be seen in this example, the initial set of information
had the tap point on the driven element too close to the center of
the element. The program went through the calculations until a
suitable tap point was found. Each time through the calculations,
the tap point and impedance were displayed to show the progression. Finally, the program reached a point where the increments
were changed to 0.25 inch until the final point was reached. Once
the correct point was found, the frequency was changed to show

how the same physical conditions could provide a suitable match at a different frequency. As it turns out, at the new frequency of 21 megahertz, only one tap point increment was required. Note the difference between the values for the gamma capacitor.

OMEGA MATCH

The Omega Match is also a method of matching antennas to transmission lines. In addition to the series capacitor and gamma rod of the Gamma Match, another capacitor is added in parallel across the open end of the Omega rod (see Fig. 4-8). Though a seemingly uncalled for addition to the Gamma Match, the added capacitor allows a person to set the tap point at one spot permanently. Therefore, instead of trying to move the tap point to find the correct matching point, the tap is set at a single spot and the two capacitors are adjusted for a suitable match. Some may deem this an unnecessary complication with little to be gained. However, depending upon the size and installation of the antenna, it may be much easier to settle for the additional capacitor rather than to try to change the gamma rod tap point. This is especially true when the tap point is out greater than three feet from the center of the element. Plus, it is relatively easy to attach a small motor to the capacitors to provide complete, remote tuning capabilities.

The program for the Omega Match is very similar to the previous Gamma Match program. In fact, it is essentially identical up through line 200. At this point, a new factor is added, C. The Omega capacitor, since it is in parallel with the short-circuited transmission line added directly to the reactance presented by this line. The value of C is either incremented or decremented until a suitable match is found.

Electrically, the Omega Match functions essentially as the Gamma Match. For the Omega Match to be effective, though, the tap point must intentionally be set closer to the center of the driven element than would normally be required for a Gamma Match; i.e., if the normal tap point for a Gamma Match was at 25 inches, the

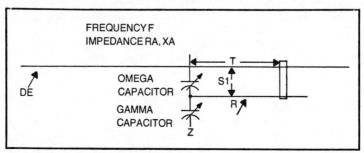

Fig. 4-3. The additional capacities which distinguish the omega match from the gamma match.

Omega Match would require that the point be set less than 25 inches. The closer the tap point is to the correct point for a Gamma Match, the smaller will be the value required for the Omega capacitor. In effect, by setting the tap point closer to the center, you are adding a large amount of inductive reactance due to the short-circuited transmission line effect. By placing the Omega capacitor across the open end of this transmission line you will be able to "tune out" the effects of the transmission line reactance. This essentially allows you to match the antenna via two capacitors.

The formulas used in the Omega Match program are the same as those used for the Gamma Match and won't be repeated.

Omega Match Program

```
1 ' OMEGA MATCH
2 CLS
3 PRINT"THIS PROGRAM WILL DETERMINE THE VALUES FOR THE SHUNT"
4 PRINT"AND SERIES CAPACITORS IN AN OMEGA MATCH."
9 PRINT
10 INPUT "ENTER DIAMETER OF ELEMENT";DE
20 INPUT "ENTER DIAMETER OF GAMMA ROD";DR
30 INPUT "ENTER SPACING BETWEEN ELEMENT AND ROD";S1
40 INPUT "ENTER TRANSMISSION SYSTEM IMPEDANCE";Z
50 INPUT "ENTER RESISTIVE PORTION OF ANTENNA IMPEDANCE";RA
60 INPUT "ENTER REACTIVE PORTION OF ANTENNA IMPEDANCE";XA
70 INPUT "ENTER FREQUENCY IN MEGAHERTZ";F
80 INPUT "ENTER DISTANCE IN INCHES FROM CENTER OF DRIVEN
ELEMENT TO SHORTING STRAP";T
85 S=DE/2+DR/2+S1
90 X=((4*S*S)-(DE↑2)+(DR↑2))/(4*S*DR):X1=LOG(X+SQR(X*X-1))
100 Y=((4*S*S)+(DE↑2)-(DR↑2))/(4*S*DE):Y1=LOG(Y+SQR(Y*Y-1))
110 HZ=(1+X1/Y1)↑2
120 ZL1=((4*S*S)-(DR↑2)-(DE↑2))/(2*DE*DR):ZL=60*(LOG(ZL1+SQR(ZL1*ZL1-1))
130 RI=HZ*RA/(COS(T*F*5.323343E-04))↑2:XI=HZ*XA/(COS(T*F*5.323343E-04))↑2
140 RI(1)=RI:XI(1)=(ZL*TAN(T*F*5.323343E-04))+XI
```

109

```
150 RI(2)=ZL-(XI*TAN(T*F*5.323343E-04)):XI(2)=RI*TAN(T*F*5.323343E-04)
160 M1=((RI(1))↑2+(XI(1))L2)↑.5:A1=ATN(XI(1)/RI(1))*57.2958
170 M2=((RI(2))↑2+(XI(2))L2)↑.5:A2=ATN(XI(2)/RI(2))*57.2958
180 M3=M1/M2:A3=A1-A2
190 RR=M3*COS(A3*.017453329):XR=(M3*SIN(A3*.017453329))
200 RS=RR:XS=XR:C=1
210 M4=1/((XS↑2+RS↑2)↑.5:A4=-ATN(XS/RS)*57.2958
220 RP=M4*COS(A4*.017453329):XP=M4*SIN(A4*.017453329)
230 XT=XP+(-1/TAN(T*F*5.323343E-04))+(2*3.1416*1E-06*F*ZL*C)
240 M5=1/((RP↑2+XT↑2)L.5:A5=-ATN(XT/RP)*57.2958
250 RS(1)=M5*COS(A5*.017453329):XS(1)=M5*SIN(A5*.017453329)
260 RF=ZL*RS(1):XF=ZL*XS(1):PRINTRF;"OHMS"
261 IF ABS(RF-Z)/Z<Z/100 GOTO 268 ELSE IF RF>Z THEN C=C-1:GOTO 230ELSE
    C=C+1:GOTO 230
268 IF C=0 PRINT"THE TAP POINT IS AT THE CORRECT SPOT FOR A GAM
    MA MATCH.  AN OMEGA CAPACITOR IS NOT NECESSARY.  THE GAMMA
    CAPACITOR IS";1E6/(2*3.1416*F*XF);"PICOFARADS.":GOTO 352
269 IF C<0 PRINT"THE TAP POINT IS TOO FAR OUT FOR AN OMEGA MATC
    H.  TRY THE COMPUTATIONS AGAIN WITH ANOTHER TAP POINT.":GOTO
    352
270 PRINT"THE FINAL RESISTANCE IS";RF"(A DIFFERENCE OF LESS THA
    N 1"CHR#(13)"PERCENT).  THE TAP POINT IS AT";T"INCHES.  THE
    GAMMA CAPACITOR"CHR#(13)"IS"1E6/(2*3.1416**F*XF);"PICOFARAD
    S.  THE OMEGA CAPACITOR IS";C;"PICOFARADS."
```

110

```
350 PRINT"AGAIN?  (1=YES, 0=NO)":INPUT Q
351 IF Q=0 THEN END
352 PRINT"ENTER THE PARAMETER YOU WANT TO CHANGE"
353 PRINTTAB(10)"ELEMENT DIAMETER       1"
354 PRINTTAB(10)"ROD DIAMETER           2"
355 PRINTTAB(10)"SPACING                3"
356 PRINTTAB(10)"SYSTEM IMPEDANCE       4"
357 PRINTTAB(10)"ANTENNA RESISTANCE     5"
358 PRINTTAB(10)"ANTENNA REACTANCE      6"
359 PRINTTAB(10)"FREQUENCY              7"
360 PRINTTAB(10)"TAP POINT              8"
361 INPUT N
362 IF N=1 PRINT"NEW ELEMENT DIAMETER?":INPUT DE
363 IF N=2 PRINT"NEW ROD DIAMETER?":INPUT DR
364 IF N=3 PRINT"NEW SPACING?":INPUT S1
365 IF N=4 PRINT"NEW SYSTEM IMPEDANCE?":INPUT Z
366 IF N=5 PRINT"NEW ANTENNA RESISTANCE?":INPUT RA
367 IF N=6 PRINT"NEW ANTENNA REACTANCE?":INPUT XA
368 IF N=7 PRINT"NEW FREQUENCY?":INPUT F
369 IF N=8 PRINT"NEW TAP POINT?":INPUT T
370 GOTO 85
```

111

Omega Match Example

Determine the values for the Omega and Gamma capacitors for an antenna with the following characteristics:

Driven Element Diameter	1 inch
Omega Rod Diameter	.25 inch
Spacing	4 inches
System Impedance	75 ohms
Resistive Part of Antenna Impedance	30 ohms
Reactive Part of Antenna Impedance	−30 ohms
Frequency	25 Megahertz
Tap Point Distance	24 inches

THIS PROGRAM WILL DETERMINE THE VALUES FOR THE SHUNT AND SERIES CAPACITORS IN AN OMEGA MATCH.

ENTER DIAMETER OF ELEMENT? 1
ENTER DIAMETER OF GAMMA ROD? .25
ENTER SPACING BETWEEN ELEMENT AND ROD? 4
ENTER TRANSMISSION SYSTEM IMPEDANCE? 75
ENTER RESISTIVE PORTION OF ANTENNA IMPEDANCE? 30
ENTER REACTIVE PORTION OF ANTENNA IMPEDANCE? −30
ENTER FREQUENCY IN MEGAHERTZ? 25
ENTER DISTANCE IN INCHES FROM CENTER OF DRIVEN ELEMENT TO SHORTING STRAP? 24
 83.3972 OHMS
 80.3289 OHMS
 77.4027 OHMS
 74.6119 OHMS
THE TAP POINT IS TOO FAR OUT FOR AN OMEGA MATCH. TRY THE COMPUTATIONS AGAIN WITH ANOTHER TAP POINT.
ENTER THE PARAMETER YOU WANT TO CHANGE

ELEMENT DIAMETER	1
ROD DIAMETER	2
SPACING	3
SYSTEM IMPEDANCE	4
ANTENNA RESISTANCE	5
ANTENNA REACTANCE	6
FREQUENCY	7
TAP POINT	8

? 8
NEW TAP POINT?
? 22
  67.5678 OHMS
  70.0705 OHMS
  72.6968 OHMS
  75.4535 OHMS
THE FINAL RESISTANCE IS 75.4535 (A DIFFERENCE OF
LESS THAN 1 PERCENT). THE TAP POINT IS AT 22 INCHES.
THE GAMMA CAPACITOR
IS 53.4325 PICOFARADS. THE OMEGA CAPACITOR IS 4
PICOFARADS.
AGAIN? (1=YES, 0=NO)
? 1
ENTER THE PARAMETER YOU WANT TO CHANGE

ELEMENT DIAMETER	1
ROD DIAMETER	2
SPACING	3
SYSTEM IMPEDANCE	4
ANTENNA RESISTANCE	5
ANTENNA REACTANCE	6
FREQUENCY	7
TAP POINT	8

? 8
NEW TAP POINT?
? 23
  75.3624 OHMS
THE FINAL RESISTANCE IS 75.3624 (A DIFFERENCE OF
LESS THAN 1 PERCENT). THE TAP POINT IS AT 23 INCHES.
THE GAMMA CAPACITOR
IS 54.0296 PICOFARADS. THE OMEGA CAPACITOR IS 1
PICOFARADS.
AGAIN? (1=YES, 0=NO)
? 0
READY

    This example was selected to illustrate several features of
this Omega Match program. In the first run through the data, the
program found that the tap point was too far out from the center of
the driven element. This means that the reactive element seen at
the open end of the short-circuited transmission line was capacitive
rather than inductive. This would have required a variable

inductance to act as the compensating element. Next, when the tap point was changed to 22 inches, a suitable match could be found. You'll note that the value for the Omega or parallel capacitor was extremely small. This indicated that the tap point was close to that required for a normal Gamma Match. The last run through the data was with the tap point at 24 inches. This produced a value for the Omega capacitor of 1 picofarad, illustrating the fact that as the tap point gets closer to that required for a Gamma Match, the value of the Omega capacitor gets increasingly smaller. Conversely, as the tap is moved in, the Omega capacitor gets larger.

T-PAD

The next three programs deal with three types of attenuators or pads: a T-pad, a Pi-pad, and a minimum loss pad. The T and Pi are named for their characteristic shapes. Each pad will provide a known amount of attenuation after determining the values by using the appropriate program.

Before going into the specifics of the T-pad, I do want to illustrate one useful property of attenuators that is oftentimes overlooked. In addition to providing known amounts of attenuation in a match system, pads can be used to provide impedance matching. Consider Fig. 4-4: this diagram shows a VSWR measuring device connected to some component that exhibits some amount of return loss (VSWR). Return loss is a measure of VSWR; the higher the return loss, the lower the VSWR. A return loss of zero dB is an infinite VSWR. A 1.4:1 VSWR corresponds to a return loss of approximately 15 dB.

In measuring return loss, a small amount of power is applied to the device under test. Some of this power is reflected back to the VSWR measuring device as a function of the VSWR or impedance match. The return loss is the difference, in dB, between the applied and reflected power.

Now, consider Fig. 4-5. In this case the applied power is mostly absorbed by the termination. The difference between applied and reflected power is very large, producing a high return loss. Next look at Fig. 4-6. Now, the 50-ohm load has been replaced with an open circuit. This presents an infinite mismatch, causing all the applied power to be reflected back, producing a return loss of zero dB. Finally, in Fig. 4-7, a 10-dB attenuator has been placed between the VSWR measuring device and the open. The applied power, when passing between the VSWR measuring device and the open, is attenuated 10 dB. At the open, the applied power, now down 10 dB, is reflected back. In the return path back to the VSWR measuring device, the reflected power is also attenuated by 10 dB. Therefore, the difference between the applied and reflected power is 20 dB, twice the value of the pad. Therefore, by simply inserting a 10-dB pad before the open improves the return loss from 0 to 20 dB. This corresponds to a decrease in VSWR from infinitely high to about 1.2:1.

This technique can be applied throughout circuitry to help maintain system and circuit impedance levels. Normally, in today's 50-ohm system, 50-ohm pads are used. However, nothing prevents one from designing pads for different impedance levels.

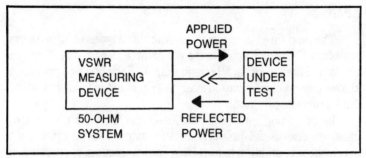

Fig. 4-4. A VSWR measuring device connected to a component which measures return loss.

Another good example is the output of a doubly balanced mixer. For best intermodulation performance, the output of the mixer should see 50-ohms for all frequencies. A pad could be inserted between the mixer and the next device to ensure a good 50-ohm termination at all frequencies. Nothing is free, however. This will only work if the system has enough gain to make up for the loss in the attenuator.

Basically, this is a very simple program. The values for the resistors are computed from the following common-day formulas:

$$R1 = Z\left(\frac{10^{.05A} - 1}{10^{.05A} + 1}\right) \quad R2 = \frac{R1\,1\,Z}{10^{.05A} - 1}$$

where Z = impedance
A = attenuation value

Once the theoretical values have been determined, the only problem is to obtain these values with practical components. The second part of the program lets you input the real values that will be used and then computes the actual attenuation.

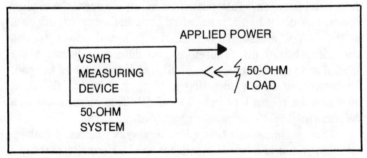

Fig. 4-5. How a VSWR measuring device with a 50 ohm load can absorb applied power.

116

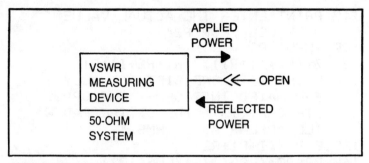

Fig. 4-6. A VSWR measuring device with the 50 ohm load replaced by an open circuit.

T-Pad Program

```
5 'T PAD CALCULATIONS
10 CLS
20 PRINT"ENTER DESIRED ATTENUATION
   VALUE"
30 INPUT A
40 PRINT"ENTER SYSTEM IMPEDANCE"
50 INPUT I
60 R1=I*((10↑(.05*A)-1)/(10↑(.05*A
   )+1))
70 R2=(R1+I)/(10↑(.05*A)-1)
80 PRINT"R1="R1"OHMS","R2="R2"OHMS
   "
90 PRINT"ENTER THE ACTUAL VALUE TO
   BE USED FOR R1"
100 INPUT R1
```

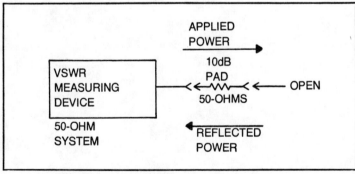

Fig. 4-7. A VSWR measuring device with a 10 dB attenuator placed between the VSWR and the open circuit.

```
110 PRINT"ENTER THE ACTUAL VALUE T
    O BE USED FOR R2"
120 INPUT R2
130 Z=(R2*(I+R1))/(R1+R2+I)+R1
140 PRINT"WITH ONE SIDE ACTUALLY T
    ERMINATED IN"I"OHMS, THE OPPOS
    ITE"CHR$(13)"SIDE OF THE PAD W
    ILL APPEAR AS"Z"OHMS."
150 E=R2/(I+R1+R2)
160 DB=20*(LOG(1/E)/LOG(10))
165 PRINT
170 PRINT"WITH R1 ="R1"OHMS AND R2
    ="R2"OHMS, THE ACTUAL ATTENUA
    TION"CHR$(13)"IS"DB"DB."
```

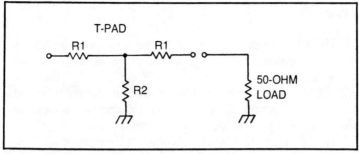

Fig. 4-8. The component designations for a 50 ohm pad with 17 dB of attenuation.

T-Pad Examples

You need a 50-ohm pad with 17 dB of attenuation. What are the required values? (See Fig. 4-8 for the component designations.)

ENTER DESIRED ATTENUATION VALUE
? 17
ENTER SYSTEM IMPEDANCE
? 50
R1 = 37.6229 OHMS   R2 = 14.413 OHMS
ENTER THE ACTUAL VALUE TO BE USED FOR R1
? 39
ENTER THE ACTUAL VALUE TO BE USED FOR R2
? 10
WITH ONE SIDE ACTUALLY TERMINATED IN 50 OHMS,
THE OPPOSITE SIDE OF THE PAD WILL APPEAR AS 47.9899 OHMS.
WITH R1 = 39 OHMS AND R2 = 10 OHMS, THE ACTUAL ATTENUATION IS 19.9127 DB.

This example readily illustrates the usefulness of this program. Since the required resistors are not of normal value, practical components have been substituted to build the T-pad. In this example, using real-world components have changed the attenuation almost 3 dB. It would be better to use a 15-ohm resistor in place of the 10-ohm resistor. This would decrease the actual attenuation to 16.8 dB vs 19.9. The impedance would also change, actually getting closer to 50 ohms.

PI-PAD

The next program covers the Pi-pad. This program is very similar to the previous T-pad program, providing the computed values and then allowing for real-world components. The best approach would be to determine the desired attenuation value and then to run both programs. From this dual information you can then select the best pad according to the components on hand.

The equations used for determination of the resistor values in the Pi-pad are:

$$R1 = Z\left(\frac{10^{.05A}+1}{10^{.05A}-1}\right) \quad R2 = \frac{Z\,R1(10^{.05A}-1)}{Z+R1}$$

Sample Pi-pad Program

```
5 'PI PAD
10 CLS
20 PRINT"ENTER DESIRED ATTENUATION
   VALUE
30 INPUT A
40 PRINT"ENTER SYSTEM IMPEDANCE"
50 INPUT Z
60 R1=Z*(10^(.05*A)+1)/(10^(.05*A)
   -1)
70 R2=Z*R1*(10^(.05*A)-1)/(Z+R1)
80 PRINT"THE REQUIRED RESISTOR FOR
   R1 IS"R1"OHMS, WHILE R2 SHOULD
   BE"R2"OHMS
90 PRINT"ENTER THE ACTUAL VALUE TO
   BE USED FOR R1"
100 INPUT RN1
110 PRINT"ENTER THE ACTUAL VALUE T
    BE USED FOR R2"
120 INPUT RN2
130 RI=(Z*(RN1+RN2)+(RN1*RN2))/(Z+
    RN1)
140 RT=R1*RI/(RI+R1)
150 PRINT"WITH ONE SIDE ACTUALLY T
    ERMINATED IN"Z"OHMS, THE OPPOS
    SIDE WILL APPEAR AS"RT"OHMS
160 E=Z*RN1/(RI*Z+RI*RN1)
```

```
170 EF=-20*(LOG(E)/LOG(10))
180 PRINT"THE ACTUAL ATTENUATION W
    ILL BE"EF"DB.
```

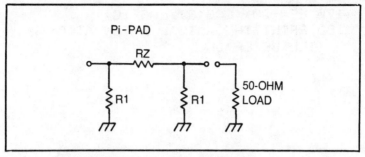

Fig. 4-9. Resistor designations required to determine the value of resistors needed for a 12 dB pad on a 600 ohm system.

Sample Pi-pad Program

What value resistors are required to make a 12-dB pad for a 600-ohm system? See Fig. 4-9 for the resistor designations.
ENTER DESIRED ATTENUATION VALUE
? 12
ENTER SYSTEM IMPEDANCE
? 600
R1 = 1 118.97   R2 = 1002.54
ENTER THE ACTUAL VALUE TO BE USED FOR R1
? 1200
ENTER THE ACTUAL VALUE TO BE USED FOR R2
? 1000
WITH ONE SIDE ACTUALLY TERMINATED IN 600 OHMS, THE OPPOSITE SIDE OF THE PAD WILL APPEAR AS 612.6 OHMS.
WITH R1 = 1200 OHMS AND R2 = 1000 OHMS, THE ACTUAL ATTENUATION IS 12 DB.

You can see from this example that as the system impedance goes higher, the pad becomes more tolerant to resistance values.

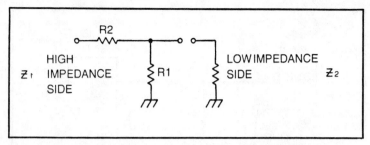

Fig. 4-10. Values for 2 resistors and their loss through the pad.

MINIMUM-LOSS PAD

The last attenuator program is a special case known as a minimum-loss pad. The pad is characterized by the ability to match impedances, whereas the T- and Pi-pad are able to swamp out impedance mismatches. However, the minimum-loss pad is also characterized by a high impedance loss through the pad. If the high loss can be tolerated, this is one excellent way of matching between two circuits. The program will provide the values for the two resistors (see Fig. 4-10 for the component designations) and the loss through the pad. The only other stipulation is that the pad is not bi-directional; it can only be installed in the circuit in one way.

The equations to determine the component values for the minimum loss pad are:

$$R1 = Z_1 (1 - Z_2/Z_1)^{\frac{1}{2}} \qquad R2 = Z_2 / (1 - (Z_2/Z_1))^{\frac{1}{2}}$$

Minimum Loss Pad Program

```
5 'MINIMUM LOSS PAD
10 CLS
20 PRINT "ENTER THE IMPEDANCES TO
   BE MATCHED (HIGH, LOW)
30 INPUT Z(1),Z(2)
40 R(1)=Z(1)*SQR(1-Z(2)/Z(1))
50 R(2)=Z(2)/SQR(1-Z(2)/Z(1))
60 PRINT"R1="R(1)"OHMS"
70 PRINT"R2="R(2)"OHMS"
80 L=LOG((Z(1)-R(1))/Z(1))/LOG(10)
90 PRINT"THE LOSS IS "20*L"DB"
```

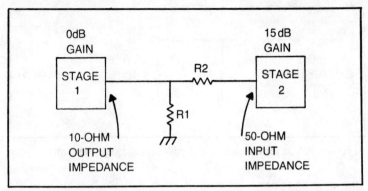

Fig. 4-11. Matching a 10 ohm output to a 50 ohm input.

Example Minimum Loss Program

As seen in Fig. 4-11, you wish to match the 10-ohm output of the first stage to the 50-ohm input of the second stage which is an rf amplifier. The amplifier has 15-dB gain. What are the values of the matching resistors and overall gain from the input of the first stage to the output of the second stage?

ENTER THE IMPEDANCES TO BE MATCHED (HIGH, LOW)
? 50,10
R1 = 44.7214 OHMS
R2 = 11.1803 OHMS
THE LOSS IS – 19.529 DB.
Overall gain, therefore, is – 4.5 dB.

PARALLEL/SERIES CONVERSIONS

As mentioned in the section of the Gamma Match program, parallel/series conversions are used during impedance transformations. There are two methods of presenting impedance data: series format and parallel format. In both cases, they consist of a real, resistive component in either series or parallel, with an imaginary, reactive component. Though the values are different, the overall impedance is still the same since this is just two different ways of presenting the same data. Generally, most information is presented in series format. However, in some cases, as in particular when paralleling components, it is easier to work with the data in a parallel format. In this way values can be added directly.

One area where this parallel presentation of impedance information is prevelant is the output of rf power transistors. In many cases manufacturers will present the transistor's input characteristics in series form and the output characteristics in a parallel form.

The equations for series/parallel conversion are:

$$R_s = \frac{R_p}{1 + \left(\dfrac{R_p}{X_p}\right)}$$

$$X_s = R_s \left(\frac{R_p}{X_p}\right)$$

$$R_p = R_s \left(1 + (X_s/R_s)^2\right)$$

$$X_p = \frac{R_p}{X_s/R_s}$$

Note that when using the plus and minus signs for the reactances they will carry through the equations to give the correct sign for the answer.

Parallel/Series Program

```
5  ' ♦ TO S AND S TO P CONVERSION
10 CLS
20 PRINT"ENTER ""S"" IF CONVERSION
   IS PARALLEL TO SERIES OR ""P""
```

```
    IF"CHR$(13)"CONVERSION IS SERI
    ES TO PARALLEL"
30 INPUT C$
40 IF C$="P"GOTO 130
50 PRINT"ENTER THE PARALLEL RESIST
   ANCE, RP (OHMS)"
60 INPUT RP
70 PRINT"ENTER THE PARALLEL REACTA
   NCE, XP (OHMS)"
80 INPUT XP
90 RS=RP/(1+(RP/XP)↑2)
100 XS=RS*RP/XP
110 PRINT"THE SERIES RESISTIVE PAR
    T IS"RS"OHMS AND THE SERIES"CH
    R$(13)"REACTIVE IS"XS"OHMS
120 END
130 PRINT"ENTER THE SERIES RESISTA
    NCE, RS (OHMS)"
140 INPUT RS
150 PRINT"ENTER THE SERIES REACTAN
    CE, XS (OHMS)"
160 INPUT XS
170 RP=RS*(1+(XS/RS)↑2)
180 XP=RP/(XS/RS)
190 PRINT"THE PARALLEL RESISTIVE P
    ART IS"RP"OHMS AND THE PARALLE
    L"CHR$(13)"REACTIVE PART IS"XP
    "OHMS
```

Parallel/Series Examples

The optimum source impedance for best noise figure of a microwave transistor is 12.5 +j0.5 ohms. What is this same impedance expressed as a parallel equivalent?

ENTER S IF CONVERSION IS PARALLEL TO SERIES OR P
IF CONVERSION IS SERIES TO PARALLEL
? P
ENTER THE SERIES RESISTANCE, RS (OHMS)
? 12.5
ENTER THE SERIES REACTANCE, XS (OHMS)
? .5
THE PARALLEL RESISTIVE PART IS 12.52 OHMS AND THE PARALLEL
REACTIVE PART IS 313 OHMS

Express 80-j90 ohms as a series equivalent.

ENTER S IF CONVERSION IS PARALLEL TO SERIES OR P
IF CONVERSION IS SERIES TO PARALLEL
? S
ENTER THE PARALLEL RESISTANCE, RP (OHMS)
? 80
ENTER THE PARALLEL REACTANCE, XP (OHMS)
? – 90
THE SERIES RESISTIVE PART IS 44.6897 OHMS AND THE SERIES
REACTIVE PART IS – 39.7241 OHMS

MATCHING NETWORKS

The four programs to follow will solve for the required reactive values in the following impedance matching networks. Since the answers are given in reactive values, they can be scaled to any frequency by using the appropriate reactance formula and frequency. The first program is for network A which is shown in Fig. 4-12.

This network is only used when the device that is to be matched has a series real part less than the load impedance. If you were to run this program several times you would see that as the real part approaches the load impedance, the reactance of C1 increases toward infinity. This network, though, can be used for RF power transistor design since their input and output impedances are generally very small.

The equations to solve network A are:

$$XL = QR + X_c$$
$$XC2 = AR_L$$

$$XC1 = \frac{(B/A)(B/Q)}{(B/A)-(B/Q)} = \frac{B}{Q-A}$$

$$\text{where } A = \sqrt{\left(\frac{R(1+Q^2)}{R_L}\right)} - 1$$

$$B = R(1+Q^2)$$

Network A Program

```
5 'MATCHING NETWORK A
10 CLS
20 PRINT"SELECT A VALUE FOR Q"
30 INPUT Q
```

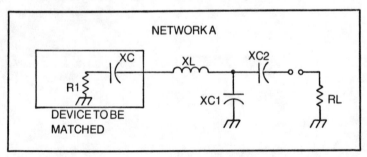

Fig. 4-12. Network A, for which Program 4-8 is designed.

```
40 PRINT"ENTER THE LOAD IMPEDANCE"
50 INPUT RL
60 PRINT"WITH THE IMPEDANCE TO BE
   MATCHED IN A SERIES FORMAT, ENT
   ER"CHR$(13)"THE RESISTIVE (OHMS
   ) AND REACTIVE ELEMENTS (OHMS).
   "
70 INPUT R,XC
80 M=SQR((R*(1+Q↑2)/RL)-1)
90 N=R*(1+Q↑2)
100 XL(1)=Q*R+XC
110 XC(1)=N/(Q-M)
120 XC(2)=M*RL
130 PRINT"XL="XL(1)"OHMS"
140 PRINT"XC1="XC(1)"OHMS"
150 PRINT"XC2="XC(2)"OHMS"
```

Network A Example

Using the diagram shown in Fig. 4-13, determine the reactance values for the matching components.

SELECT A VALUE FOR Q
? 3
ENTER THE LOAD IMPEDANCE
? 75
WITH THE IMPEDANCE TO BE MATCHED IN A SERIES FORMAT, ENTER THE RESISTIVE (OHMS) AND REACTIVE ELEMENTS (OHMS).
? 20, −30
XL = 30 OHMS
XC1 = 117.027 OHMS
XC2 = 96.8246 OHMS
READY

You'll notice that, in this example, the reactance of the inductor matches the reactance of the output capacitance. In this way, the reactive element is cancelled and the two capacitors transform the real part of the output impedance up to the 75-ohm load impedance.

To illustrate the problem encountered with a series real part close the load impedance, run the following information: Q = 3, ZL = 75, Real Part = 74, and Imaginary Part = −30

SELECT A VALUE FOR Q
? 3
ENTER THE LOAD IMPEDANCE
? 75
WITH THE IMPEDANCE TO BE MATCHED IN A SERIES FORMAT, ENTER THE RESISTIVE (OHMS) AND REACTIVE ELEMENTS (OHMS).
? 74, −30

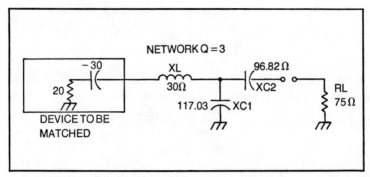

Fig. 4-13. Network Q-3, to be used in Network A problem.

XL = 192 OHMS
XC1 = 33177.5 OHMS
XC2 = 223.327 OHMS

When applied to the standard capacitive reactance formula, the 33000+ ohms create a very small capacitor value.

Network B Example

Network B, as shown in Fig. 4-14 is the Pi network which has been widely used to match the output of a vacuum-tube transmitter to a transmission line.

The main limitation of this network deals with the selection of Q and the matching range. When a low Q is selected, the value of the parallel real part of the output impedance must also be low. This will be illustrated in the following examples. Notice that the program calls for the data to be input in a series equivalent format. If you wish to use the series format, delete line 71. Otherwise, leave line 71 in and input the data in a parallel format. The type of format you use will depend generally upon the device being matched. For example, some power transmitters present their output impedance data in a parallel equivalent, while others use a series equivalent format. Power tubes, on the other hand, use a parallel format.

The equations to solve for the required component values are:

$$XC1 = R/Q$$

$$XC2 = RL\sqrt{\frac{R/RL}{(Q^2+1)-(R/RL)}}$$

$$XL = \frac{QR + (RRL/XC2)}{Q^2 + 1}$$

Network B Program

```
5 'MATCHING NETWORK B
10 CLS
20 PRINT"SELECT A VALUE FOR Q"
```

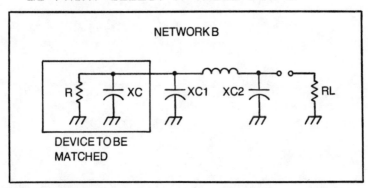

Fig. 4-14. Network B, for which Program 4-9 is designed.

132

```
30 INPUT Q
40 PRINT"ENTER THE LOAD IMPEDANCE"
50 INPUT RL
60 PRINT"WITH THE IMPEDANCE TO BE
   MATCHED IN A SERIES FORMAT, ENT
   ER"CHR$(13)"THE RESISTIVE (OHMS
   ) AND REACTIVE ELEMENTS (OHMS).
   "
70 INPUT R,XC
71 RP=R:XP=XC:GOTO 100
80 RP=R*(1+(XC/R)↑2)
90 XP=RP/(XC/R)
100 XC(1)=RP/Q
110 XC(2)=RL*SQR((RP/RL)/((Q↑2+1)-
    (RP/RL)))
120 XL=(Q*RP+(RP*RL/XC(2)))/(Q↑2+1
    )
130 PRINT"XC1="XC(1)"OHMS"
140 PRINT"XC2="XC(2)"OHMS"
150 PRINT"XL="XL"OHMS"
```

Sample Network B Problems

Match the output of the vacuum tube transmitter shown in Fig. 4-15 using a network with a Q of 5 and a load impedance of 50 ohms. (Since the diagram shows the output in a parallel format, leave line 71 in the program.)

SELECT A VALUE FOR Q

? 5

ENTER THE LOAD IMPEDANCE

? 50

WITH THE IMPEDANCE TO BE MATCHED IN A SERIES FORMAT, ENTER THE RESISTIVE (OHMS) AND REACTIVE ELEMENTS (OHMS).

? 2000, 10

?FC ERROR IN 110

This example shows that with the high real part of the impedance to be matched and with the low Q of the network, there is no solution to the problem. To achieve a solution, the circuit Q will have to be raised.

SELECT A VALUE FOR Q

? 15

ENTER THE LOAD IMPEDANCE

? 50

WITH THE IMPEDANCE TO BE MATCHED IN A SERIES FORMAT, ENTER THE RESISTIVE (OHMS) AND REACTIVE ELEMENTS (OHMS).

? 2000, 10

XC1 = 133.333 OHMS

XC2 = 23.1869 OHMS

XL = 151.826 OHMS

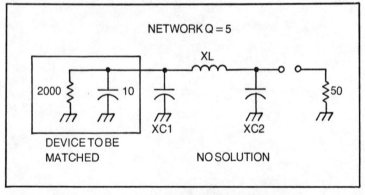

Fig. 4-15. Network Q-5, to be used in Network B problem.

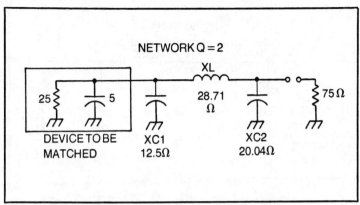

Fig. 4-16. Network Q-2, to be used in Network B problem.

In actual practice, the value for C1 = C1 − Output C. Depending upon the frequency and the matching components, C1 can actually be eliminated and the output capacitance of the tube will suffice for the matching capacitor. This, generally, happens only at frequencies greater than 40 to 50 megahertz.

Match the output impedance of the circuit shown in Fig. 4-16 to 50 ohms using a network with a Q of 2.

SELECT A VALUE FOR Q
? 2
ENTER THE LOAD IMPEDANCE
? 75
WITH THE IMPEDANCE TO BE MATCHING IN A SERIES FORMAT, ENTER THE RESISTIVE (OHMS) AND REACTIVE ELEMENTS (OHMS).
? 25,5
XC1 = 12.5 OHMS
XC2 = 20.0446 OHMS
XL = 28.7083 OHMS

Network C

Network C can be implemented by either of the two methods shown in Fig. 4-17.

This program, though, is designed to solve for the matching network when the data is presented in a series equivalent format. In either case, the real part of the impedance to be matched must be less than the load impedance. Practically, this configuration yields the best component values when the real part is of a low value.

The equations to solve network C are:

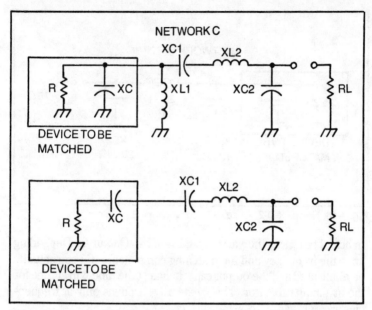

Fig. 4-17. Two methods by which Network C can be implemented.

$$XL1 = XC$$
$$XC1 = QR$$
$$XC2 = RL \sqrt{\frac{R1}{RL - R}}$$
$$XL2 = XC1 + \left(\frac{RRL}{XC2}\right)$$

Parallel Format

$$XC1 = QR1$$
$$XC2 = RL \sqrt{\frac{R}{RL - R}}$$
$$XL2 = XC1 + \left(\frac{RRL}{XC2}\right) + XC$$

Series Format

Network C Program

```
5  'MATCHING NETWORK C
10 CLS
20 PRINT"SELECT A VALUE FOR Q"
```

136

```
30  INPUT Q
40  PRINT"ENTER THE LOAD IMPEDANCE"
50  INPUT RL
60  PRINT"WITH THE IMPEDANCE TO BE
    MATCHED IN A SERIES FORMAT, ENT
    ER"CHR$(13)"THE RESISTIVE (OHMS
    ) AND REACTIVE ELEMENTS (OHMS).
    "
70  INPUT R,XC
100 XC(1)=R*Q
110 XC(2)=RL*SQR(R/(RL-R))
120 XL(1)=XC(1)+(R*RL/XC(2))+XC
130 PRINT"XL="XL(1)"OHMS"
140 PRINT"XC1="XC(1)"OHMS"
150 PRINT"XC2="XC(2)"OHMS"
```

Sample Network C Programs

Match the circuit shown in Fig. 4-18 using Network C with a Q of 5.

SELECT A VALUE FOR Q
? 3
ENTER THE LOAD IMPEDANCE
? 50
WITH THE IMPEDANCE TO BE MATCHED IN A SERIES FORMAT, ENTER THE RESISTIVE (OHMS) AND REACTIVE ELEMENTS (OHMS).
? 60,300
? FC ERROR IN 110
READY

This illustrates the point that the load impedance must be higher than the series real part. Now, try solving the network by raising the load impedance to 75 ohms

SELECT A VALUE FOR Q
? 3
ENTER THE LOAD IMPEDANCE
? 75
WITH THE IMPEDANCE TO BE MATCHED IN A SERIES FORMAT, ENTER THE RESISTIVE (OHMS) AND REACTIVE ELEMENTS (OHMS).
? 60,300
XL = 510 OHMS
XC1 = 180 OHMS
XC2 = 150 OHMS
READY

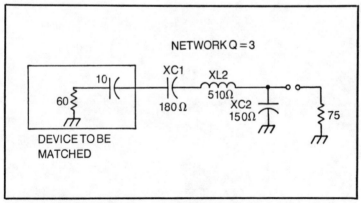

Fig. 4-18. Network Q-3, to be used in Network C problem.

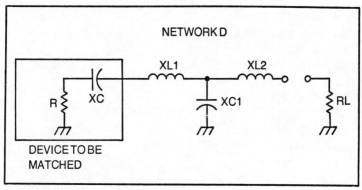

Fig. 4-19. Network D.

Network D

The last program covers Network D, the classical T type of network. An illustration of Network D is given in Fig. 4-19. The advantage of this network is that it will match load impedances that are both less than and greater than the series real part of the impedance to be matched.

Equations to use this network are:

$$XL1 = RQ + XC$$
$$XL2 = RLB$$

$$XC1 = \frac{A}{Q + B}$$

where $A = R(1 + Q^2)$

$$B = \sqrt{\left(\frac{A}{RL}\right) - 1}$$

Network D Program

```
5 'MATCHING NETWORK D
10 CLS
20 PRINT"SELECT A VALUE FOR Q"
30 INPUT Q
40 PRINT"ENTER THE LOAD IMPEDANCE"
50 INPUT RL
60 PRINT"WITH THE IMPEDANCE TO BE
    MATCHED IN A SERIES FORMAT, ENT
    ER"CHR$(13)"THE RESISTIVE (OHMS
    ) AND REACTIVE ELEMENTS (OHMS).
```

139

```
70  INPUT R,XC
80  M=R*(1+Q↑2)
90  N=SQR(M/RL-1)
100 XL(1)=R*Q+XC
110 XL(2)=RL*N
120 XC=M/(Q+N)
130 PRINT"XL1="XL(1)"OHMS"
140 PRINT"XL2="XL(2)"OHMS"
150 PRINT"XC="XC"OHMS"
```

Sample Network D Problems

Match the circuit shown in Fig. 4-20A by using network D. The load impedance is 50 ohms and the circuit Q is 10.

SELECT A VALUE FOR Q

? 10

ENTER THE LOAD IMPEDANCE

? 50

WITH THE IMPEDANCE TO BE MATCHED IN A SERIES FORMAT, ENTER THE RESISTIVE (OHMS) AND REACTIVE (OHMS) ELEMENTS.

? 5,10

XL1 = 60 OHMS

XL2 = 150.831 OHMS

XC = 38.7966 OHMS

Match the circuit shown in Fig. 4-20B to a load impedance of 50 ohms using network D with a circuit Q of 10.

SELECT A VALUE FOR Q

? 10

ENTER THE LOAD IMPEDANCE

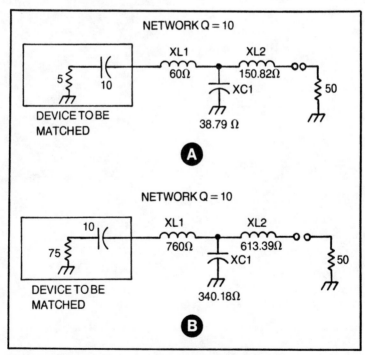

Fig. 4-20. Network Q-10, to be used in Network D problem.

141

? 50
WITH THE IMPEDANCE TO BE MATCHED IN A SERIES
FORMAT, ENTER THE RESISTIVE (OHMS) AND REACTIVE
ELEMENTS (OHMS).
? 75,10
XL1 = 760 OHMS
XL2 = 613.392 OHMS
XC = 340.177 OHMS
This illustrates that, regardless of the value of the series real part,
the T network is able to perform the necessary matching.

CAPACITIVE-DIVIDER NETWORK

The last network to be discussed is the capacitive-divider transformer. This network uses a resonant circuit to match between a low and high impedance. Whereas the minimum loss pad had considerable loss, this circuit exhibits only minimal loss. In addition, since a tuned circuit is used, it shows a band pass characteristic and is therefore useful in minimizing harmonic energy. Since specific frequencies are used for the center frequency and bandwidth, the solution provided by this program is a listing of real component values rather than reactances.

To solve the capacitive-divider transformer manually, use the following equations and Fig. 4-21:

$$Q = \frac{\text{Center Freq.}}{\text{Bandwidth}}$$

$$CT = \frac{Q}{2\pi\, 1 = \left(\dfrac{RL}{2}\right)} \times 10^6$$

$$C2/C1 = \sqrt{\frac{RL}{R} - 1}$$

$$CT = \frac{C1 \times C2}{C1 + C2}$$

Capacitive-Divider Network Program

```
5 'CAPACITIVE DIVIDER TRANSFORMER
10 CLS
20 PRINT"ENTER LOAD IMPEDANCE (>50
   OHMS)"
30 INPUT RL
40 PRINT"ENTER CENTER FREQUENCY (M
   HZ)"
```

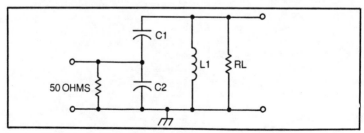

Fig. 4-21. A C-D Transformer.

```
50 INPUT F
60 PRINT"ENTER BANDWIDTH (MHZ)"
70 INPUT B
80 Q=F/B
90 CT=Q*1E6/(2*3.1416*F*(RL/2))
100 M=SQR(RL/50)-1
110 C1=CT/(M/(M+1))
120 C2=M*C1
130 L=1/(4*3.1416↑2*F↑2*CT*1E-6)
150 PRINT"C1="C1"PICOFARADS"
160 PRINT"C2="C2"PICOFARADS"
170 PRINT"L="L"MICROHENRYS"
```

Example Capacitive-Divider Network Problem

Using the capacitive-divider transformer network shown in Fig. 4-22, determine the required component values for a bandwidth of 250 kHz at a center frequency of 10 MHz.

ENTER LOAD IMPEDANCE (>50 OHMS)
? 500
ENTER CENTER FREQUENCY (MHZ)
? 10
ENTER BANDWIDTH (MHZ)
? .250
C1 = 3724.15 PICOFARADS
C2 = 8052.66 PICOFARADS
L = .0994715 MICROHENRYS

As proof, determine the resonant frequency of the tuned circuit by:

$$f = \frac{1}{2\pi \sqrt{LC}}$$

where C = series capacitance of C1 and C2

$$f = \frac{1}{\sqrt{2\pi \ .099 \times 10^{-6} \cdot 2.55 \times 10^{-9}}}$$

$$f = \frac{.159}{\sqrt{2.52 \times 10^{-16}}} = \frac{.159}{1.59 \times 10^{-8}} = 10.01 \text{ MHz}$$

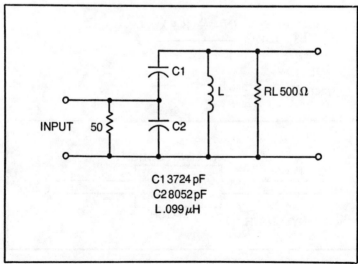

C1 3724 pF
C2 8052 pF
L .099 μH

Fig. 4-22. C-D transformer network to be used in example problem.

SERIES-MATCHING SECTION

This next program uses a rather unusual matching technique known as the series-matching section. Because of the materials involved, it is more applicable to matching antennas rather than circuits. This technique uses a group of different impedance transmission lines matching different impedances. To understand, see Fig. 4-23; this diagram illustrates that two different impedance sections of transmission line are inserted between the system transmission line and the load to be matched.

The program computes the lengths of the matching sections in electrical degrees. For practical implementation, the velocity factor constant will have to be applied to find the physical lengths. Using real transmission lines the different impedance values that can be matched are somewhat limited, however, there is enough range to match most real-world type of requirements. At higher frequencies where stripline and microstrip construction are prevalent, the impedance of the transmission line can be tailored to fit the needs of the matching problem.

The equations used to determine the length of the matching sections are:

$$L2 = \tan^{-1} \sqrt{\frac{(R-1)^2 + X^2}{R(N - \frac{1}{N})^2 (R-1)^2 - X^2}} = B$$

$$L1 = \tan^{-1} \frac{(N - \frac{R}{N} B + X}{R + XNB - 1} = A$$

where $N = \dfrac{Z \, match}{Z \, line}$

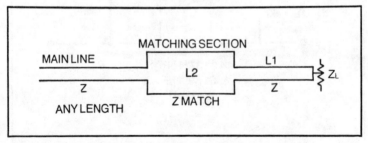

Fig. 4-23. A series-matching section illustrating two difference impedance sections of transmission line.

$$R = \frac{RL}{Z_o}$$

$$X = \frac{XL}{Z_o}$$

In some cases, the values of impedance for the matching section and main line section are too close together. This may cause the quantity under the radical to be negative, an invalid solution. The limits on the impedance of the transmission line can be calculated by the following formulas:

$$Z_{match} > Z_{line} \sqrt{SWR} \text{ or } Z_{match} < Z_{line} \sqrt{SWR}$$
FOR MATCHING TO OCCUR

The program automatically calculates these limits and gives an error message when the values are too close.

Series Section Program

```
5 'SERIES MATCHING SECTION
10 CLS
20 PRINT"ENTER LOAD IMPEDANCE (R,X
   )
30 INPUT R,X
40 PRINT"ENTER THE IMPEDANCE OF TH
   E MAIN LINE"
50 INPUT Z(1)
60 PRINT"ENTER THE IMPEDANCE OF TH
   E MATCHING SECTION"
70 INPUT Z(2)
71 S=SQR(R♦2+X♦2)/Z(1)
72 IF S<1 THEN S=1/S
75 GOTO 110
80 N=Z(2)/Z(1)
90 R=R/Z(1)
100 X=X/Z(1)
105 GOTO 125
110 IF Z(2)>Z(1)*SQR(S) OR Z(2)<Z(
    1)/SQR(S)GOTO 120 ELSE PRINT"I
    NSUFFICIENT RANGE FOR MATCHINGI
    .  CHOOSE A NEW VALUE FOR THE"
    CHR$(13)"MATCHING SECTION"
```

```
115 GOTO 20
120 GOTO 80
125 ON ERROR GOTO 190
130 B=SQR(((R-1)♦2+(X♦2))/(R*(N-1/
    N)♦2-(R-1)♦2-(X♦2)))
140 A=((N-R/N)*B+X)/(R+X*B*N-1)
150 IF ATN(A)*57.29578<0 THEN L1=A
    TN(A)*57.29578+180 ELSE L1=ATN
    (A)*57.29578
160 L2=ATN(B)*57.29578
170 PRINT"SECTION 1 --"L1"DEGREES"
180 PRINT"SECTION 2 --"L2"DEGREES"
185 END
190 PRINT"INSUFFICIENT RANGE FOR M
    ATCHING.  CHOOSE A NEW VALUE F
    OR"CHR$(13)"THE MATCHING SECTI
    ON.":GOTO 60
```

Series Matching Section Examples

Match the antenna shown in Fig. 4-24 with a series matching section to a 50-ohm transmission line. The impedance of the matching section is 75 ohms.

ENTER LOAD IMPEDANCE (R,X)
? 250,100
ENTER THE IMPEDANCE OF THE MAIN LINE
? 50
ENTER THE IMPEDANCE OF THE MATCHING SECTION
? 75
INSUFFICIENT RANGE FOR MATCHING. CHOOSE A NEW VALUE FOR THE MATCHING SECTION
ENTER LOAD IMPEDANCE (R,X)
? 250,100
ENTER THE IMPEDANCE OF THE MATCHING SECTION
? 93
INSUFFICIENT RANGE FOR MATCHING. CHOOSE A NEW VALUE FOR THE MATCHING SECTION.
ENTER LOAD IMPEDANCE (R,X)
? 250,100
ENTER THE IMPEDANCE OF THE MAIN LINE
? 50
ENTER THE IMPEDANCE OF THE MATCHING SECTION
? 300
SECTION 1 — 24.8774 DEGREES
SECTION 2 — 20.051 DEGREES

This example shows that you would have to use a section of 300-ohm balanced line to match the load. This might present some practical problems, interfacing between the 50-ohm unbalanced and 300-ohm balanced lines. However, it illustrates the wide range of antenna matching that can be achieved by using the series-matching section.

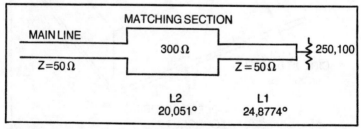

Fig. 4-24. Antenna to be used in solving the series-matching section problem.

MICROSTRIP

The last program in this chapter is used to determine the width of microstrip transmission lines for specific values of impedance. As I mentioned in the previous section, the microstrip transmission lines can be tailored in impedance to fulfill the matching requirements. In many other cases, the impedance of the microstrip is also tailored to meet the matching requirements, i.e., low noise microwave amplifiers or vhf/uhf power amplifiers.

Figure 4-25 illustrates the relationships that are used in this program. The microstrip is that portion of the copper cladding that is not etched away. To compute the width of the microstrip, two different formulas are used. Once the width is determined, the correct answer is chosen according to the width-to-height ratio. Lines 60 through 90 perform the actual computations for the two formulas, while line 180 determines which answer of the two to use.

The two formulas to calculate the width of the microstrip are:

$$w/h < 2 \qquad w/h = \frac{8 e^{A}}{e^{2A} - 2}$$

$$w/h > 2 \qquad w/h = \frac{2}{\pi} \left(B - 1 - (n(2B-1) + \frac{E_r - 1}{Z_{E_r}} \right.$$

$$\left. (1n(B-1) + .39 - \frac{.61}{E_r} \right) \right)$$

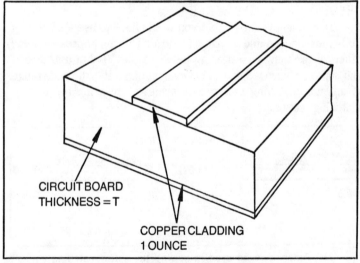

CIRCUIT BOARD
THICKNESS = T

COPPER CLADDING
1 OUNCE

Fig. 4-25. The relationships used in the microstrip program.

$$\text{where } A = \frac{Z_0}{60} \sqrt{\frac{E_r+1}{2}} + \frac{E_r-1}{E_r+1}\left(.23 + \frac{.11}{E_r}\right)$$

$$B = \frac{377\pi}{2Z_0 \sqrt{E_r}}$$

Microstrip Program

```
5 'MICROSTRIP CALCULATIONS
10 CLS
20 PRINT"ENTER DESIRED IMPEDANCE O
   F MICROSTRIP"
30 INPUT Z
40 PRINT"ENTER DIELECTRIC CONSTANT
   OF CIRCUIT BOARD MATERIAL"
50 INPUT E
55 GOTO 100
60 A=(Z/60)*SQR((E+1)/2)+((E-1)/(E
   +1))*(.11/E+.23)
70 B=592.1902/(Z*SQR(E))
80 WH(1)=8*2.7183+A/(2.7183+(2*A)-
   2)
90 WH(2)=.6366*((B-1)-LOG(2*B-1)+(
   (E-1)/(2*E))*(LOG(B-1)+.39-.61/
   E))
95 GOTO 140
100 PRINT"ENTER THICKNESS OF CIRCU
    IT BOARD (MILS)
110 INPUT T
120 PRINT"ENTER THICKNESS OF COPPE
    R (OUNCES)
130 INPUT O
135 GOTO 60
140 O=O*1.4
150 H=T-2*O
160 R=WH(1)*H
170 S=WH(2)*H
180 IF WH(1)<2 PRINT"THE MICROSTRI
    P IS"R"MILS WIDE" ELSE PRINT"T
    HE MICROSTRIP IS"S"MILS WIDE"
```

Microstrip Examples

Determine the width of a 50-ohm line on a glass epoxy board that is 1/16-inch thick. The copper clad is 1 ounce.

ENTER DESIRED IMPEDANCE OF MICROSTRIP
? 50
ENTER DIELECTRIC CONSTANT OF CIRCUIT BOARD MATERIAL
? 5 (Glass epoxy)
ENTER THICKNESS OF CIRCUIT BOARD (MILS)
? 62
ENTER THICKNESS OF COPPER (OUNCES)
? 1
THE MICROSTRIP IS 102.721 MILS WIDE.

Next, compute the width of the same microstrip except on an alumina substrate.

ENTER DESIRED IMPEDANCE OF MICROSTRIP
? 50
ENTER DIELECTRIC CONSTANT OF CIRCUIT BOARD MATERIAL
? 8.8
ENTER THICKNESS OF CIRCUIT BOARD (MILS)
? 62
ENTER THICKNESS OF COPPER (OUNCES)
? 1
THE MICROSTRIP IS 63.8949 MILS WIDE.

This illustrates that as the dielectric constant of the circuit board material is raised, the lines can be of smaller width. By using substrates with a higher dielectric constant, microwave circuitry can be reduced significantly in size as compared to lower frequency type of circuits.

Chapter 5
Geometry

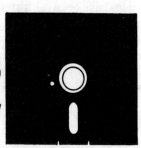

This last chapter is not a return to the eighth grade. However, it is devoted to the person who uses his computer for the more exotic problems. The first group of programs in this chapter will deal with the hyperbolic functions which are used in a lot of engineering problems. In addition, hyperbolic functions are quite useful in connection with differential equations.

HYPERBOLIC FUNCTIONS

The basic identities of the hyperboic sine and cosine are related to the coordinates of the points X, Y on the basic hyperbola $X^2 - Y^2 = 1$. Sinh and Cosh, the hyperboic sine and cosine, respectively, are identified as follows:

$$\text{Sinh } X = \tfrac{1}{2}(e^x - e^{-x})$$
$$\text{Cosh } X = \tfrac{1}{2}(e^x + e^{-x})$$

The remaining hyperbolic functions are defined in terms of sinh x and cosh x as follows:

$$\tanh X = \frac{\sinh X}{\cosh X}$$

$$\coth X = \frac{\cosh X}{\sinh X}$$

$$\text{sech } X = \frac{1}{\cosh X}$$

$$\text{csch } X = \frac{1}{\sinh X}$$

The graphs of the hyperbolic functions are shown in Figs. 5-1 through 5-6. The hyperbolic cosine is an even function, cosh(−x) = cosh x, and the hyperbolic sine is an odd function, sinh(−x) = −sinh x. Therefore, one curve is symmetrical about the y-axis and the other is symmetrical with respect to the origin. Here, the hyperbolic functions behave like ordinary trigonometric functions.

The hyperbolic functions are so important that their numerical values have been calculated and tabulated just as have the ordinary trigonometric functions. However, it is very inconvenient to have to stop work and look up a value in a table. Thus, the reason for the following six programs. In this way they can be incorporated directly into a program. As a good example, the impedance of the transmission line in the Gamma and Omega programs was calculated using the hyperbolic cosine.

Hyperbolic Sine Program

```
5 'HYPERBOLIC SINE
10 CLS
20 PRINT"ENTER X FOR HYPERBOLIC SI
   NE (SINH) OF X"
30 INPUT X
40 A=((EXP(1)♦X)-(EXP(1)♦-X))/2
50 PRINT"THE HYPERBOLIC SINE OF"X"
   IS"A
```

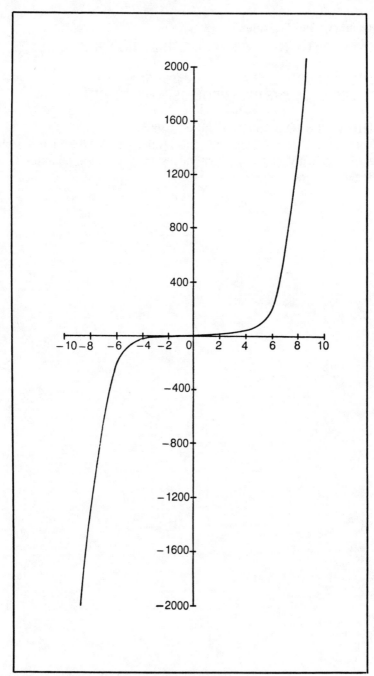

Fig. 5-1. A graph illustrating the hyperbolic sine.

Hyperbolic Sine Examples

ENTER X FOR THE HYPERBOLIC SINE (SINH) OF X
? 9
THE HYPERBOLIC SINE OF 9 IS 4051.54
ENTER X FOR THE HYPERBOLIC SINE (SINH) OF X
? .6
THE HYPERBOLIC SINE OF .6 IS .636654
Note from Fig. 5-1 that with small values of X, the sinh is correspondingly small, greater values of X produce infinitely larger numbers.

Hyperbolic Cosine Program

```
5 'HYPERBOLIC COSINE
10 CLS
20 PRINT"ENTER X FOR HYPERBOLIC CO
   SINE (COSH) OF X"
30 INPUT X
40 A=((EXP(1)↑X)+(EXP(1)↑-X))/2
50 PRINT"THE HYPERBOLIC COSINE OF"
   X"IS"A
```

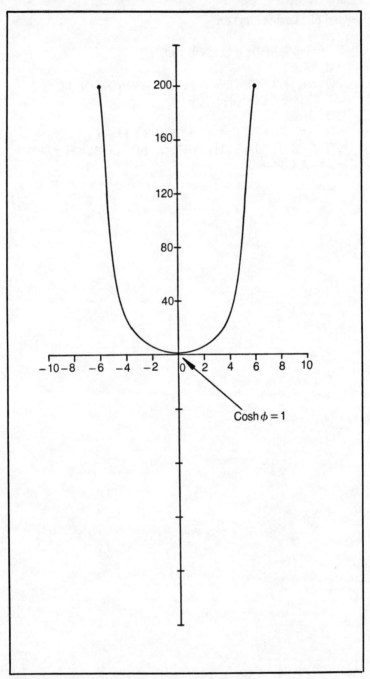

Fig. 5-2. A graph illustrating the hyperbolic cosine.

Hyperbolic Cosine Examples

ENTER X FOR HYPERBOLIC COSINE (COSH) OF X
? -3
THE HYPERBOLIC COSINE OF -3 IS 10.0677
ENTER X FOR HYPERBOLIC COSINE (COSH) OF X
? 0
THE HYPERBOIC COSINE OF 0 IS 1

You'll note that this example shows that the minimum value the hyperbolic cosine can assume is 1. Figure 5-2 also illustrates this fact, showing that the curve is symmetrical about the Y axis.

Hyperbolic Tangent Program

```
5 'HYPERBOLIC TANGENT
10 CLS
20 PRINT"ENTER X FOR HYPERBOLIC TA
   NGENT (TANH) OF X"
30 INPUT X
40 A=((EXP(1)^X)-(EXP(1)^-X))/((EX
   P(1)^X)+(EXP(1)^-X))
50 PRINT"THE HYPERBOLIC TANGENT OF
   "X"IS"A
```

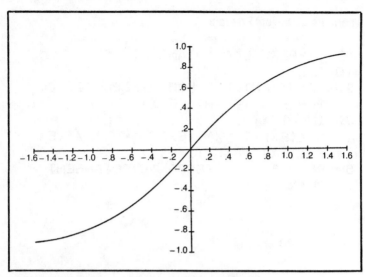

Fig. 5-3. A graph illustrating the hyperbolic tangent.

Hyperbolic Tangent Examples

ENTER X FOR HYPERBOLIC TANGENT (TANH) OF X
? 2
THE HYPERBOLIC TANGENT OF 2 IS .964028

As you run a hyperbolic tangent you'll find that it quickly approaches, but never reaches, 1. The TRS-80 is limited in the number of digits it can display. Even using double precision will only allow you to compute a hyperbolic tangent of about 8.3. To use double precision, change lines A in lines 40 and 50 to A#.

161

Hyperbolic Cotangent Program

```
 5 'HYPERBOLIC COTANGENT
10 CLS
20 PRINT"ENTER X FOR HYPERBOLIC CO
   TANGENT (COTH) OF X"
30 INPUT X
40 A=((EXP(1)♦X)+(EXP(1)♦-X))/((EX
   P(1)♦X)-(EXP(1)♦-X))
50 PRINT"THE HYPERBOLIC COTANGENT
   OF"X"IS"A
```

Hyperbolic Cotangent Examples

ENTER X FOR HYPERBOLIC COTANGENT (COTH) OF X
? IE-7
THE HYPERBOLIC COTANGENT OF 1E-07 IS 5.59241E+06
ENTER X FOR HYPERBOLIC COTANGENT (COTH) OF X
? 5
THE HYPERBOLIC COTANGENT OF 5 IS 1.00009

From these examples and Fig. 5-4 you can see that as the hyperbolic cotangent approaches zero, its value becomes infinitely big, and it approaches 1 as X becomes large.

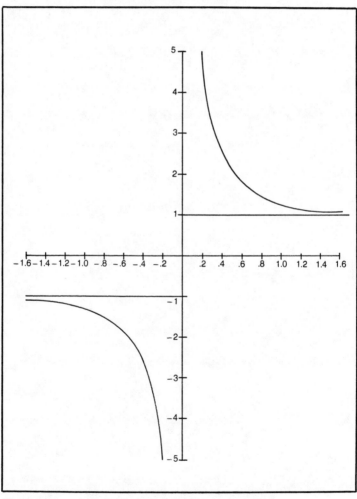

Fig. 5-4. A graph illustrating the hyperbolic cotangent.

Hyperbolic Secant Program

```
 5 'HYPERBOLIC SECANT
10 CLS
20 PRINT"ENTER X FOR HYPERBOLIC SE
   CANT (SECH) OF X"
30 INPUT X
40 A=2/((EXP(1)^X)+(EXP(1)^-X))
50 PRINT"THE HYPERBOLIC SECANT OF"
   X"IS"A
```

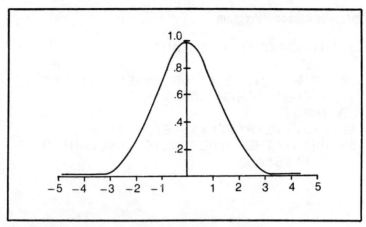

Fig. 5-6. A graph illustrating the hyperbolic secant.

Hyperbolic Secant Examples

ENTER X FOR HYPERBOLIC SECANT (SECH) OF X
? 0
THE HYPERBOLIC SECANT OF 0 IS 1
ENTER X FOR HYPERBOLIC SECANT (SECH) OF X
? 50
THE HYPERBOLIC SECANT OF 50 IS 3.8575E-22

The maximum value for the hyperbolic secant is one. As X gets increasingly big, either positive or negative, the hyperbolic secant approaches zero.

Generally, the hyperbolic functions behave much like $e^X/2$, $e^{-X}/2$, unity, or zero as shown in the following table:

X (Large and Positive)	X Negative, |X| Large
$\cosh X \approx \sinh x$	$\cosh X \approx -\sinh X$
$\approx \frac{1}{2}e^x$	$\approx \frac{1}{2}e^{-x}$
$\tanh X \approx \coth X \approx 1$	$\tanh X \approx \coth \approx -1$
$\operatorname{sech} X \approx \operatorname{csch} \approx$	$\operatorname{sech} X \approx -\operatorname{csch} X$
$\approx 2e^{-x} \approx 0$	$\approx 2e^x \approx 0$

Hyperbolic Cosecant Program

```
5 'HYPERBOLIC COSECANT
10 CLS
20 PRINT"ENTER X FOR HYPERBOLIC CO
   SECANT (CSCH) OF X"
30 INPUT X
40 A=2/((EXP(1)^X)-(EXP(1)^-X))
50 PRINT"THE HYPERBOLIC COSECANT O
   F"X"IS"A
```

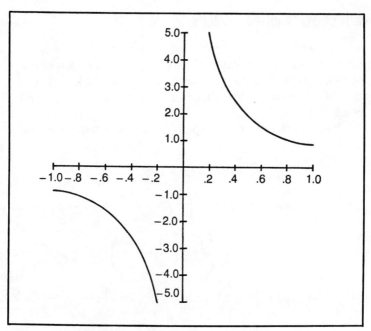

Fig. 5-5. A graph illustrating the hyperbolic cosecant.

Hyperbolic Cosecant Examples

ENTER X FOR HYPERBOLIC COSECANT (CSCH) OF X
? 2
THE HYPERBOLIC COSECANT OF 2 IS .275721
ENTER X FOR THE HYPERBOLIC COSECANT (CSCH) OF X
? –2
THE HYPERBOLIC COSECANT OF –2 IS –.275721

The hyperbolic cosecant is very similar to the hyperbolic cotangent, except that instead of being asymptotic to Y=1 it is asymptotic to Y=0. Again, as the value of X gets smaller, the hyperbolic cosecant becomes infinitely big.

INVERSE HYPERBOLIC FUNCTIONS

The inverse hyperbolic functions perform the inverse operation of the hyperbolic functions. That is, if you compute $X = \sinh Y$, then the inverse hyperbolic secant is $Y = \sinh^{-1} X$. The general curves for the inverse hyperbolic functions are shown in Fig. 5-7 through 5-12.

To compute the inverse hyperbolic functions, use the following formulas:

$$\sinh^{-1} x = \ln(x + (x^2 + 1)^{.5})$$

$$\tanh^{-1} x = \tfrac{1}{2}(n\left(\frac{1+x}{1-x}\right)$$

$$\operatorname{sech}^{-1} x = \ln\left(\frac{1}{x} + \left(\frac{1}{x^2} - 1\right)^{.5}\right)$$

$$\cosh^{-1} x^2 = \operatorname{sech}^{-1} \frac{1}{x}$$

$$\coth^{-1} x^2 = \operatorname{tcnh}^{-1} \frac{1}{x}$$

$$\operatorname{csch}^{-1} x^2 = \sinh^{-1} \frac{1}{x}$$

Inverse Hyperbolic Sine Program

```
5 'INV. HYPERBOLIC SINE
10 CLS
20 PRINT"ENTER X FOR INVERSE HYPER
   BOLIC SINE OF X"
30 INPUT X
40 A=LOG(X+((X↑2)+1)↑.5)
50 PRINT"THE INVERSE HYPERBOLIC SI
   NE OF"X"IS"A
```

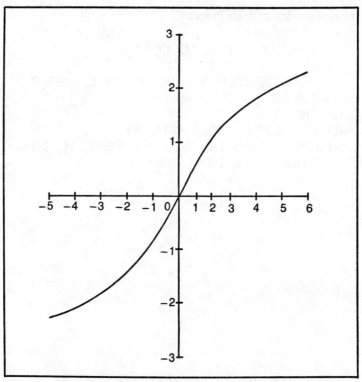

Fig. 5-7. A graph illustrating the inverse hyperbolic sine.

Inverse Hyperbolic Sine Examples

ENTER X FOR INVERSE HYPERBOLIC SINE OF X
? 5
THE INVERSE HYPERBOLIC SINE OF 5 IS 2.3124
ENTER X FOR INVERSE HYPERBOLIC SINE OF X
? – 5
THE INVERSE HYPERBOLIC SINE OF – 5 IS – 2.3124

These examples show that the inverse hyperbolic sine is a single value; that is, as X varies, Y produces a different answer for each value of X. The curve does not reverse to produce the same value for X as for – X.

Inverse Hyperbolic Cosine Program

```
5 'INV. HYPERBOLIC COSINE
10 CLS
20 PRINT"ENTER X FOR INVERSE HYPER
   BOLIC COSINE OF X"
30 INPUT X
40 A=LOG(X+((X[2)-1)↑.5)
50 PRINT"THE INVERSE HYPERBOLIC CO
   SINE OF"X"IS"A 45B=-A
```

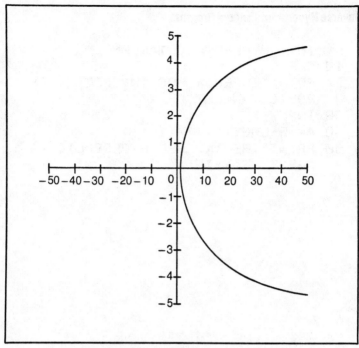

Fig. 5-8. A graph illustrating the inverse hyperbolic cosine.

Inverse Hyperbolic Cosine Examples

ENTER X FOR INVERSE HYPERBOLIC COSINE OF X
? .5
?FC ERROR IN 40
Whereas cosh $\emptyset = 1$, the inverse hyperbolic function is limited to the range of greater than one.
ENTER X FOR INVERSE HYPERBOLIC COSINE OF X
? 20
THE INVERSE HYPERBOLIC COSINE OF 20 IS 3.68825 AND -3.68825
Note that in the solution for the inverse hyperbolic cosine, for each value of X there are two corresponding values for Y.

Inverse Hyperbolic Tangent Program

```
5 'INV. HYPERBOLIC TANGENT
10 CLS
20 PRINT"ENTER X FOR INVERSE HYPER
   BOLIC TANGENT OF X"
30 INPUT X
40 A=.5*LOG((1+X)/(1-X))
50 PRINT"THE INVERSE HYPERBOLIC TA
   NGENT OF"X"IS"A
```

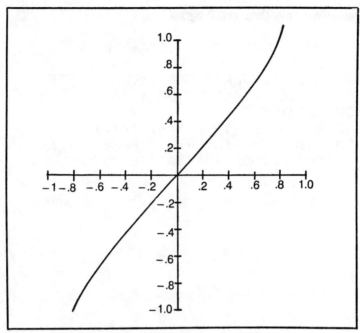

Fig. 5-9. A graph illustrating the inverse hyperbolic tangent.

Inverse Hyperbolic Tangent Examples

ENTER X FOR INVERSE HYPERBOLIC TANGENT OF X
? .4
THE INVERSE HYPERBOLIC TANGENT OF .4 IS .423649
ENTER X FOR INVERSE HYPERBOLIC TANGENT OF X
? .1
THE INVERSE HYPERBOLIC TANGENT OF .1 IS .100335

You'll note from these two examples and the curve shown in Fig. 5-9 that the inverse hyperbolic tangent is *almost* a straight-line function. However, as X approaches 1, the function becomes asymptotic to at the X = 1 and X = −1 lines.

Inverse Hyperbolic Cotangent Program

```
5 'INV. HYPERBOLIC COTANGENT
10 CLS
20 PRINT"ENTER X FOR INVERSE HYPER
   BOLIC COTANGENT OF X"
30 INPUT X
40 A=.5*LOG((1+1/X)/(1-1/X))
50 PRINT"THE INVERSE HYPERBOLIC CO
   TANGENT OF"X"IS"A
```

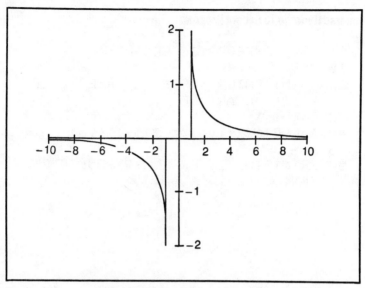

Fig. 5-10. A graph illustrating the inverse hyperbolic cotangent.

Inverse Hyperbolic Cotangent Examples

ENTER X FOR INVERSE HYPERBOLIC COTANGENT OF X
?.5
?FC ERROR IN 40
This shows that the function $Y = \coth^{-1} X$ is only valid for X greater
than 1 and X less than -1. The region running from -1 through 0 to
1 is invalid.
ENTER X FOR INVERSE HYPERBOLIC COTANGENT OF X
?-6
THE INVERSE HYPERBOLIC COTANGENT OF -6 IS
$-.168236$

Inverse Hyperbolic Secant Program

```
5 'INV. HYPERBOLIC SECANT
10 CLS
20 PRINT"ENTER X FOR INVERSE HYPER
   BOLIC SECANT OF X"
30 INPUT X
40 A=LOG(1/X+(((1/X↑2))-1)↑.5)
45 B=-A
50 PRINT"THE INVERSE HYPERBOLIC SE
   CANT OF"X"IS"A"AND" B
```

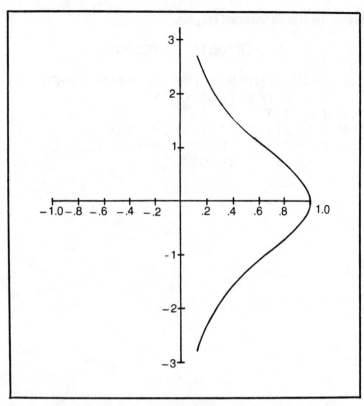

Fig. 5-11. A graph illustrating the inverse hyperbolic secant.

Inverse Hyperbolic Secant Examples

ENTER X FOR INVERSE HYPERBOLIC SECANT OF X
? 1
THE INVERSE HYPERBOLIC SECANT OF 1 IS Ø
ENTER X FOR INVERSE HYPERBOLIC SECANT OF X
? .6
THE INVERSE HYPERBOLIC SECANT OF .6 IS 1.09861 AND
−1.09861

The inverse hyperbolic secant acts in the same manner as the inverse hyperbolic cosine. Each unique value of X produces two answers, Y and −Y. Small values of X eventually become asymptotic to the Y axis, both plus and minus (see Fig. 5-11).

Inverse Hyperbolic Cosecant Program

```
5 'INV. HYPERBOLIC COSECANT
10 CLS
20 PRINT"ENTER X FOR INVERSE HYPER
   BOLIC COSECANT OF X"
30 INPUT X
40 A=LOG(1/X+(((1/X*2))+1)*.5)
50 PRINT"THE INVERSE HYPERBOLIC CO
   SECANT OF"X"IS"A
```

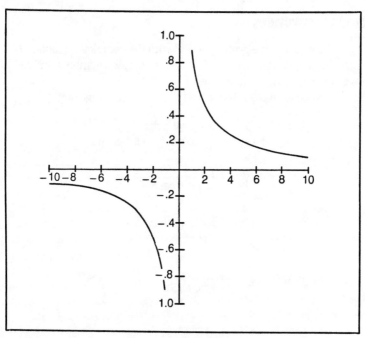

Fig. 5-12. A graph illustrating the inverse hyperbolic cosecant.

Inverse Hyperbolic Cosecant Examples

ENTER X FOR INVERSE HYPERBOLIC COSECANT OF X
? 0
?/ Ø   ERROR IN 40
ENTER X FOR INVERSE HYPERBOLIC COSECANT OF X
? 8
THE INVERSE HYPERBOLIC COSECANT OF 8 IS .124677

    The curve of the inverse hyperbolic cosecant is not unlike the curve of the inverse hyperbolic cotangent. However, instead of small values of X becoming asymptotic to X = 1, the curve is asymptotic to the Y axis. Large values of X eventually become asymptotic to the X axis (see Fig. 5-12).

COMPLEX FUNCTIONS

The next twelve programs deal with the complex trigonometric functions, or the sine, cosine, . . . of complex numbers and the inverse trigonometric functions.

The equations to solve each of the following programs are:

$$\sin(x + iy) = \sin x \cosh Y + i \cos x \sinh Y$$
$$\cos(x + iY) = \cos x \cosh Y - i \sin x \sinh Y$$

$$\tan(x + iy) = \frac{\sin 2x + i \sinh 2Y}{\cos 2x + \cosh 2Y}$$

$$\cot(x + iy) = \frac{\sin 2x - i \sinh 2Y}{\cosh 2x - \cos 2Y}$$

$$\csc(x + iy) = \frac{1}{\sin(x + iY)}$$

$$\sec(x + iy) = \frac{1}{\cos(x + iY)}$$

$$\sin^{-1}(x + iy) = \sin^{-1} B + i \operatorname{sgn}(y) \ln(A + \sqrt{A^2 - 1})$$

where

$$A = \tfrac{1}{2} \sqrt{(X + 1)^2 + y^2} + \tfrac{1}{2} \sqrt{(c - 1)^2 + y^2}$$

$$B = \tfrac{1}{2} \sqrt{(X + 1)^2 + y^2} - \tfrac{1}{2} \sqrt{(c - 1)^2 + y^2}$$

$$\operatorname{sgn}(Y) = 1 \text{ if } y \geq 0$$
$$\qquad\quad -1 \text{ if } y < 0$$
$$\cos^{-1}(x + iy) = \cos^{-1} B + i \operatorname{sgn}(d) \ln(A + \sqrt{A^2 - 1})$$

where

$$A = \tfrac{1}{2} \sqrt{(x + 1)^2 + y^2} + \tfrac{1}{2} \sqrt{(c - 1)^2 + y^2}$$

$$B = \tfrac{1}{2} \sqrt{(x + 1)^2 + y^2} - \tfrac{1}{2} \sqrt{(c - 1)^2 + y^2}$$
$$\operatorname{sgn}(Y) = 1 \text{ if } y \geq 0$$
$$\qquad\quad -1 \text{ if } y < 0$$

$$\tan^{-1}(x+iy) = \tfrac{1}{2}\left(\pi - \tan^{-1}\frac{1+y}{A} - \tan^{-1}\frac{1-B}{A}\right) + \frac{\iota}{4}$$
$$\ln\left(\frac{(1+y)^2 + x^2}{(1-y)^2 + x^2}\right)$$

$$\cot^{-1}(x+iy) = \frac{\pi}{2} - \tan^{-1}(x+iy)$$

$$\csc^{-1}(x+iy) = \sin^{-1}\left(\frac{1}{x+iy)}\right)$$

$$\sec^{-1}(x+iy) = \cos^{-1}\left(\frac{1}{x+iy}\right)$$

Complex Sine Program

```
5 'COMPLEX SINE
10 CLS
20 PRINT"ENTER COMPLEX NUNBER (REA
   L,IMAGINARY)"
30 INPUT R,I
40 AR=SIN(R)*((EXP(1)↑I+EXP(1)↑-I)
   /2)
50 AI=COS(R)*((EXP(1)↑I-EXP(1)↑-I)
   /2)
60 PRINT"THE COMPLEX SINE IS"AR;AI
   "I"
```

Complex Sine Examples

ENTER COMPLEX NUMBER (REAL, IMAGINARY)
? 2, −3
THE COMPLEX SINE IS 9.1545 4.16891
ENTER COMPLEX NUMBER (REAL, IMAGINARY)
? 3, −4
THE COMPLEX SINE IS 3.85374 27.0168

Complex Cosine Program

```
5 'COMPLEX COSINE
10 CLS
20 PRINT"ENTER COMPLEX NUMBER (REA
   L,IMAGINARY)"
30 INPUT R,I
40 AR=COS(R)*((EXP(1)↑I+EXP(1)↑-I)
   /2)
50 AI=-(SIN(R)*((EXP(1)↑I-EXP(1)↑-
   I)/2))
60 PRINT"THE COMPLEX COSINE IS"AR;
   AI"I"
```

Complex Cosine Examples

ENTER COMPLEX NUMBER (REAL, IMAGINARY)
? 2, −3
THE COMPLEX COSINE IS 4.18963 9.10923
ENTER COMPLEX NUMBER (REAL, IMAGINARY)
? −.2, 5
THE COMPLEX COSINE IS 72.7307 14.7419

Complex Tangent Program

```
5  'COMPLEX TANGENT
10 CLS
20 PRINT"ENTER COMPLEX NUNBER (REA
   L,IMAGINARY)"
30 INPUT R,I
40 D=COS(2*R)+((EXP(1)^(2*I)+EXP(1
   )^(2*-I))/2)
50 AR=SIN(2*R)/(D)
60 AI=((EXP(1)^(2*I)+EXP(1)^(2*-I)
   )/2)/(D)
70 PRINT"THE COMPLEX TANGENT IS"AR
   ;AI"i"
```

Complex Tangent Examples

ENTER COMPLEX NUMBER (REAL, IMAGINARY)
? – 2, – 3
THE COMPLEX TANGENT IS 3.76403E-03 1.00325
ENTER COMPLEX NUMBER (REAL, IMAGINARY)
? 10, – 5
THE COMPLEX TANGENT IS 8.28923E-05 .999963

Complex Cotangent Program

```
5 'COMPLEX COTANGENT
10 CLS
20 PRINT"ENTER COMPLEX NUNBER (REA
   L,IMAGINARY)"
30 INPUT R,I
40 D=-COS(2*R)+((EXP(1)^(2*I)+EXP(
   1)^(2*-I))/2)
50 AR=SIN(2*R)/(D)
60 AI=-((EXP(1)^(2*I)-EXP(1)^(2*-I
   ))/2)/(D)
70 PRINT"THE COMPLEX COTANGENT IS"
   AR;AI"i"
```

Complex Cotangent Examples

ENTER COMPLEX NUMBER (REAL, IMAGINARY)
? 2,3
THE COMPLEX COTANGENT IS 3.73971E-03 -.996758
ENTER COMPLEX NUMBER (REAL, IMAGINARY)
? -12, .3
THE COMPLEX CONTANGENT IS 1.18954 - .836285

Complex Secant Program

```
  5 'COMPLEX SECANT
 10 CLS
 20 PRINT"ENTER COMPLEX NUNBER (REA
    L,IMAGINARY)"
 30 INPUT R,I
 40 AR=COS(R)*((EXP(1)♦I+EXP(1)♦-I)
    /2)
 50 AI=-(SIN(R)*((EXP(1)♦I-EXP(1)♦-
    I)/2))
 60 M=SQR(AR[2+AI♦2)
 70 T=ATN(AI/AR)
 80 FR=1/M*(COS(-T))
 90 FI=1/M*(SIN(-T))
100 PRINT"THE COMPLEX SECANT IS"FR
    ;FI
```

Complex Secant Examples

ENTER COMPLEX NUMBER (REAL, IMAGINARY)
? 4, −9
THE COMPLEX SECANT IS 1.61332E-04 −1.86794E-04
ENTER COMPLEX NUMBER (REAL, IMAGINARY)
? −.009, 10
THE COMPLEX SECANT IS 9.07961E-05 −8.17201E-07

Complex Cosecant Program

```
5 'COMPLEX COSECANT
10 CLS
20 PRINT"ENTER COMPLEX NUNBER (REA
   L,IMAGINARY)"
30 INPUT R,I
40 AR=SIN(R)*((EXP(1)↑I+EXP(1)↑-I)
   /2)
50 AI=COS(R)*((EXP(1)↑I-EXP(1)↑-I)
   /2)
60 M=SQR(AR[2+AI↑2)
70 T=ATN(AI/AR) -
80 FR=1/M*(COS(-T))
90 FI=1/M*(SIN(-T))
100 PRINT"THE COMPLEX COSECANT IS"
    FR;FI
```

Complex Cosecant Examples

ENTER COMPLEX NUMBER (REAL, IMAGINARY)
? 3, – .5
THE COMPLEX COSECANT IS .545987 – 1.77002
? – .3, 10
THE COMPLEX COSECANT IS 2.68332E-05 8.67444E-05

Complex Arc Sine Program

```
5 'COMPLEX ARC SINE
10 CLS
20 PRINT"ENTER COMPLEX NUMBER (REA
   L, IMAGINARY)
30 INPUT R,I
40 M=SQR((R+1)↑2+(I↑2))
50 N=SQR((R-1)↑2+(I↑2))
60 Z(1)=.5*M+.5*N
70 Z(2)=.5*-M+.5*N
80 Z(3)=.5*M+.5*-N
90 Z(4)=.5*-M+.5*-N
100 Z(5)=.5*M-.5*N
110 Z(6)=.5*-M-.5*N
120 Z(7)=.5*M-.5*-N
130 Z(8)=.5*-M-.5*-N
140 FOR P=5 TO 8
145 IF Z(P)<0 GOTO 160
146 IF Z(P)>1 GOTO 160
150 AR(P)=ATN(Z(P)/SQR(-Z(P)*Z(P)+
    1))
160 NEXT P
170 IF I=>0 THEN S=1 :STOPS=-1
180 FOR P=1 TO 4
185 IF Z(P)<1 GOTO 210
190 A1(P)=(LOG(Z(P)+SQR(Z(P)↑2-1))
    )*S
200 A2(P)=(LOG(Z(P)-SQR(Z(P)↑2-1))
    )*S
210 NEXT P
220 PRINT"THE COMPLEX ARC SINE IS
    --"
230 FOR P=5 TO 8
240 IF AR(P)=0 GOTO300
250 FOR G=1 TO 4
260 IF A1(G)=0 GOTO290
270 PRINTAR(P),A1(G)
280 PRINTAR(P),A2(G)
290 NEXT G
300 NEXT P
```

Complex Arc Sine Examples

ENTER COMPLEX NUMBER (REAL, IMAGINARY)
? 5, 8
THE COMPLEX ARC SINE IS —
.556083   2.93872
.556083   −2.93872
Note that all the inverse complex trigonometric functions are double-valued.
ENTER COMPLEX NUMBER (REAL, IMAGINARY)
? 1, −2
THE COMPLEX ARC SINE IS —
.4247079   −1.52857
.427079   1.52857

Complex Arc Cosine Program

```
5 'COMPLEX ARC COSINE
10 CLS
20 PRINT"ENTER COMPLEX NUMBER (REA
   L, IMAGINARY)
30 INPUT R,I
40 M=SQR((R+1)^2+(I^2))
50 N=SQR((R-1)^2+(I^2))
60 Z(1)=.5*M+.5*N
70 Z(2)=.5*-M+.5*N
80 Z(3)=.5*M+.5*-N
90 Z(4)=.5*-M+.5*-N
100 Z(5)=.5*M-.5*N
110 Z(6)=.5*-M-.5*N
120 Z(7)=.5*M-.5*-N
130 Z(8)=.5*-M-.5*-N
140 FOR P=5 TO 8
145 IF Z(P)<0 GOTO 160
146 IF Z(P)>1 GOTO 160
150 AR(P)=-ATN(Z(P)/SQR(-Z(P)*Z(P)
    +1))+1.5708
160 NEXT P
170 IF I=>0 THEN S=1 ELSE S=-1
180 FOR P=1 TO 4
185 IF Z(P)<1 GOTO 210
190 A1(P)=-(LOG(Z(P)+SQR(Z(P)^2-1)
    ))*S
200 A2(P)=-(LOG(Z(P)-SQR(Z(P)^2-1)
    ))*S
210 NEXT P
220 PRINT"THE COMPLEX ARC COSINE I
    S --"
230 FOR P=5 TO 8
240 IF AR(P)=0 GOTO300
250 FOR G=1 TO 4
260 IF A1(G)=0 GOTO290
270 PRINTAR(P),A1(G)
280 PRINTAR(P),A2(G)
290 NEXT G
300 NEXT P
```

Complex Arc Cosine Examples

ENTER COMPLEX NUMBER (REAL, IMAGINARY)
? 1, –2
THE COMPLEX ARC COSINE IS —
1.14372   1.52857
1.14872   –1.52857
ENTER COMPLEX NUMBER (REAL, IMAGINARY)
? 23,8
THE COMPLEX ARC COSINE IS —
.334995   –3.88541
.334995   3.88556

Complex Arc Tangent Program

```
5 'COMPLEX ARC COTANGENT
10 CLS
20 PRINT"ENTER COMPLEX NUMBER (REA
   L, IMAGINARY)
30 INPUT R,I
40 AR=.5*(3.14159-ATN((1+I)/R)-ATN
   ((1-I)/R))
50 AI=LOG(((1+I)[2+R[2)/((1-I)↑2+R
   ↑2))/4
60 PRINT"THE COMPLEX ARC COTANGENT
    IS --"
70 PRINT3.14159/2-AR,AI
```

Complex Arc Tangent Examples

ENTER COMPLEX NUMBER (REAL, IMAGINARY)
? 5, 8
THE COMPLEX ARC TANGENT IS —
1.51422   .0898434
1.51422   −.0898434

Complex Arc Cotangent Program

```
5  'COMPLEX ARC COTANGENT
10 CLS
20 PRINT"ENTER COMPLEX NUMBER (REA
   L, IMAGINARY)
30 INPUT R,I
40 AR=.5*(3.14159-ATN((1+I)/R)-ATN
   ((1-I)/R))
50 AI=LOG(((1+I)[2+R[2)/((1-I)♦2+R
   ♦2))/4
60 PRINT"THE COMPLEX ARC COTANGENT
    IS --"
70 PRINT3.14159/2-AR,AI
```

Complex Arc Cotangent Examples

ENTER COMPLEX NUMBER (REAL, IMAGINARY)
? 2, 3
THE COMPLEX ARC COTANGENT IS —
.160875   − .229073
.160875   .229073
ENTER COMPLEX NUMBER (REAL, IMAGINARY)
? 1, 1
THE COMPLEX ARC COTANGENT IS —
.553574   .40236
.553574   − .40236

Complex Arc Secant Program

```
5 'COMPLEX ARC SECANT
10 CLS
20 PRINT"ENTER COMPLEX NUMBER (REAL,
   IMAGINARY)
30 INPUT R,I
35 GOSUB 310
40 M=SQR((R+1)[2+(I[2))
50 N=SQR((R-1)[2+(I[2))
60 Z(1)=.5*M+.5*N
70 Z(2)=.5*-M+.5*N
80 Z(3)=.5*M+.5*-N
90 Z(4)=.5*-M+.5*-N
100 Z(5)=.5*M-.5*N
110 Z(6)=.5*-M-.5*N
120 Z(7)=.5*M-.5*-N
130 Z(8)=.5*-M-.5*-N
140 FOR P=5 TO 8
145 IF Z(P)<0 GOTO 160
146 IF Z(P)>1 GOTO 160
150 AR(P)=-ATN(Z(P)/SQR(-Z(P)*Z
    (P)+1))+1.5708
160 NEXT P
170 IF I=>0 THEN S=1 ELSE S=-1
180 FOR P=1 TO 4
185 IF Z(P)<1 GOTO 210
190 A1(P)=-(LOG(Z(P)+SQR(Z(P)♦2-1)))*S
200 A2(P)=-(LOG(Z(P)-SQR(Z(P)♦2-1)))*S
210 NEXT P
220 PRINT"THE COMPLEX ARC SECANT IS --
230 FOR P=5 TO 8
240 IF AR(P)=0 GOTO300
250 FOR G=1 TO 4
260 IF A1(G)=0 GOTO290
270 PRINTAR(P),A1(G)
280 PRINTAR(P),A2(G)
290 NEXT G
300 NEXT P
305 END
310 F=SQR(R[2+I[2)
```

```
320 T=ATN(I/R)
330 F=1/F
340 T=-T
350 R=F*COS(T)
360 I=F*SIN(T)
370 RETURN
```

Complex Arc Secant Examples

ENTER COMPLEX NUMBER (REAL, IMAGINARY)
? 8,−5
THE COMPLEX ARC SECANT IS −
1.48093   −.0563788
1.48093   .0563784
ENTER COMPLEX NUMBER (REAL, IMAGINARY)
? −.03, .03
THE COMPLEX ARC SECANT IS −
.785853 −3.85313
.785853   3.85321

Complex Arc Cosecant

```
5 'COMPLEX ARC COSECANT
10 CLS
20 PRINT"ENTER COMPLEX NUMBER (REA
   L, IMAGINARY)
30 INPUT R,I
35 GOSUB 310
40 M=SQR((R+1)♦2+(I♦2))
50 N=SQR((R-1)♦2+(I♦2))
60 Z(1)=.5*M+.5*N
70 Z(2)=.5*-M+.5*N
80 Z(3)=.5*M+.5*-N
90 Z(4)=.5*-M+.5*-N
100 Z(5)=.5*M-.5*N
110 Z(6)=.5*-M-.5*N
120 Z(7)=.5*M-.5*-N
130 Z(8)=.5*-M-.5*-N
140 FOR P=5 TO 8
145 IF Z(P)<0 GOTO 160
146 IF Z(P)>1 GOTO 160
150 AR(P)=ATN(Z(P)/SQR(-Z(P)*Z(P)÷
    1))
160 NEXT P
170 IF I=>0 THEN S=1 ELSE S=-1
180 FOR P=1 TO 4
185 IF Z(P)<1 GOTO 210
190 A1(P)=(LOG(Z(P)+SQR(Z(P)♦2-1))
    )*S
200 A2(P)=(LOG(Z(P)-SQR(Z(P)♦2-1))
    )*S
210 NEXT P
220 PRINT"THE COMPLEX ARC COSECANT
     IS --"
230 FOR P=5 TO 8
240 IF AR(P)=0 GOTO300
250 FOR G=1 TO 4
260 IF A1(G)=0 GOTO290
270 PRINTAR(P),A1(G)
280 PRINTAR(P),A2(G)
290 NEXT G
300 NEXT P
```

```
305 END
310 F=SQR(R[2+I[2)
320 T=ATN(I/R)
330 F=1/F
340 T=-T
350 R=F*COS(T)
360 I=F*SIN(T)
370 RETURN
```

Complex Arc Cosecant Examples

? 5, 8
THE COMPLEX ARC COSECANT IS —
.0559826   −.089909
.0559826   .0899086
ENTER COMPLEX NUMBER (REAL, IMAGINARY)
? −2, 3
THE COMPLEX ARC COSECANT IS —
.150386   .231335
.150386   −.231335

COMPLEX HYPERBOLIC FUNCTIONS

The last group of trigonometric function programs are the complex hyperbolic functions. Programs to solve the complex hyperbolic functions are:

$\sinh(x + iY) = -i \sin i (x + iY)$
$\cosh(x + iY) = \cos i (x + iy)$
$\tanh(x + iY) = -i \tan i (x + iY)$
$\coth(x + iY) = i \cot i (x + iY)$
$\operatorname{csch}(x + iy) = i \csc i (x + iY)$
$\operatorname{sech}(x + iy) = \sec i (x + iY)$

Complex Hyperbolic Sine Program

```
5 'COMPLEX HYPERBOLIC SINE
10 CLS
20 PRINT"ENTER COMPLEX NUMBER (REA
   L,IMAGINARY)"
30 INPUT I,R
40 AR=SIN(R)*((EXP(1)↑I+EXP(1)↑-I)
   /2)
50 AI=COS(R)*((EXP(1)↑I-EXP(1)↑-I)
   /2)
60 PRINT"THE COMPLEX HYPERBOLIC SI
   NE IS"AI;AR"I"
```

Complex Hyperbolic Sine Examples

ENTER COMPLEX NUMBER (REAL, IMAGINARY)
? 3,3
THE COMPLEX HYPERBOLIC SINE IS – 9.91762 1.42075
ENTER COMPLEX NUMBER (REAL, IMAGINARY)
? –3, –3
THE COMPLEX HYPERBOLIC SINE IS 9.91762 –1.42075

```
5 'COMPLEX HYPERBOLIC COSINE
10 CLS
20 PRINT"ENTER COMPLEX NUNBER (REA
   L,IMAGINARY)"
30 INPUT I,R
40 AR=COS(R)*((EXP(1)♦I+EXP(1)♦-I)
   /2)
50 AI=(SIN(R)*((EXP(1)♦I-EXP(1)♦-I
   )/2))
60 PRINT"THE COMPLEX HYPERBOLIC CO
   SINE IS"AR;AI"I"
```

Complex Hyperbolic Cosine Examples

ENTER COMPLEX NUMBER (REAL, IMAGINARY)
0 3, 2
THE COMPLEX HYPERBOLIC COSINE IS −4.18963   9.10923
ENTER COMPLEX NUMBER (REAL, IMAGINARY)
0 2, 3
THE COMPLEX HYPERBOLIC COSINE IS −3.72455   .511823

Complex Hyperbolic Tangent Programs

```
5 'COMPLEX HYPERBOLIC TANGENT
10 CLS
20 PRINT"ENTER COMPLEX NUNBER (REA
   L,IMAGINARY)"
30 INPUT I,R
40 D=COS(2*R)+((EXP(1)↑(2*I)+EXP(1
   )↑(2*-I))/2)
50 AR=SIN(2*R)/(D)
60 AI=((EXP(1)↑(2*I)+EXP(1)↑(2*-I)
   )/2)/(D)
70 PRINT"THE COMPLEX HYPERBOLIC TA
   NGENT IS"AI;AR"I"
```

Complex Hyperbolic Tangent Examples

ENTER COMPLEX NUMBER (REAL, IMAGINARY)
? 1,2
THE COMPLEX HYPERBOLIC TANGENT IS 1.21027
−.243458
ENTER COMPLEX NUMBER (REAL, IMAGINARY)
? 5,−3
THE COMPLEX HYPERBOLIC TANGENT IS .999913
2.53687E-05

```
5 'COMPLEX HYPERBOLIC COTANGENT
10 CLS
20 PRINT"ENTER COMPLEX NUNBER (REA
   L,IMAGINARY)"
30 INPUT I,R
40 D=COS(2*R)-((EXP(1)♦(2*I)+EXP(1
   )♦(2*-I))/2)
50 AR=SIN(2*R)/(D)
60 AI=-((EXP(1)♦(2*I)-EXP(1)♦(2*-I
   ))/2)/(D)
70 PRINT"THE COMPLEX HYPERBOLIC CO
   TANGENT IS"AI;AR"i"
```

Complex Hyperbolic Cotangent Examples

ENTER COMPLEX NUMBER (REAL, IMAGINARY)
? 3,4
THE COMPLEX HYPERBOLIC COTANGENT IS .999267
−4.90118E-03
ENTER COMPLEX NUMBER (REAL, IMAGINARY)
? 1,10
THE COMPLEX HYPERBOLIC COTANGENT IS 1.08132
−.272187

```
5 'COMPLEX HYPERBOLIC SECANT
10 CLS
20 PRINT"ENTER COMPLEX NUMBER (REA
   L,IMAGINARY)"
30 INPUT I,R
40 AR=COS(R)*((EXP(1)↑I+EXP(1)↑-I)
   /2)
50 AI=-(SIN(R)*((EXP(1)↑I-EXP(1)↑-
   I)/2))
60 M=SQR(AR↑2+AI↑2)
70 T=ATN(AI/AR)
80 FR=-1/M*(COS(-T))
90 FI=1/M*(SIN(-T))
100 PRINT"THE COMPLEX HYPERBOLIC S
    ECANT IS"FR;FI
```

Complex Hyperbolic Secant Examples

ENTER COMPLEX NUMBER (REAL, IMAGINARY)
? 1, 2
THE COMPLEX HYPERBOLIC SECANT IS – .413149 – .687527
ENTER COMPLEX NUMBER (REAL, IMAGINARY)
? 2,1
THE COMPLEX HYPERBOLIC SECANT IS – .151176 .226974

This completes the programs and examples for the trigonometric functions. Though each is short, the basic equations and examples have been given to aid in understanding. Additionally, the computational part of the programs can be incorporated into larger, more complex programs.

```
5 'COMPLEX HYPERBOLIC COSECANT
10 CLS
20 PRINT"ENTER COMPLEX NUMBER (REA
   L,IMAGINARY)"
30 INPUT I,R
40 AR=SIN(R)*((EXP(1)↑I+EXP(1)↑-I)
   /2)
50 AI=COS(R)*((EXP(1)↑I-EXP(1)↑-I)
   /2)
60 M=SQR(AR↑2+AI↑2)
70 T=ATN(AI/AR)
80 FR=-1/M*(COS(-T))
90 FI=-1/M*(SIN(-T))
100 PRINT"THE COMPLEX HYPERBOLIC C
    OSECANT IS"FI;FR
```

Complex Hyperbolic Cosecant Examples

ENTER COMPLEX NUMBER (REAL, IMAGINARY)
? 4,5
THE COMPLEX HYPERBOLIC COSECANT IS −.0103816
−.0351186
ENTER COMPLEX NUMBER (REAL, IMAGINARY)
? 5, 4
THE COMPLEX HYPERBOLIC COSECANT IS 8.80791E-03
−.0101989

TRIANGLES

The next four programs in this chapter deal with solving triangle problems. They are especially useful in surveying work. Solving for the unknown sides and angles of oblique triangles depends upon using the Law of Sines and Law of Cosines which are:

$$\text{Law of Sines} - \frac{1}{\operatorname{Sin} A} = \frac{b}{\sin B} = \frac{c}{\sin C}$$

$$\text{Law of Cosines} - \quad c^2 = a^2 + b^2 - 2\,ab \cos C$$

Two Sides, Non-Included Angle Program

```
5  '2 SIDES, NON-INCLUDED ANGLE
10 CLS
20 PRINT"ENTER THE TWO SIDES AND T
   HE NON-INCLUDED ANGLE"
25 PRINT"ENTER FIRST SIDE, SECOND
   SIDE AND ITS ASSOCIATED ANGLE"
30 INPUT BS,AS,AA
31 QA=AA
35 AA=AA*.01745329
40 Z=BS*SIN(AA)/AS
50 BA=ATN(Z/SQR(-Z*Z+1))*57.29578
60 CA=180-QA-BA
65 CA=CA*.01745329
70 CS=AS*SIN(CA)/SIN(AA)
90 PRINT"THE THIRD SIDE IS"CS", IT
   S ASSOCIATED ANGLE IS"CA*57.295
   78CHR$(13)"DEGREES AND THE FIRS
   T SIDE'S ASSOCIATED ANGLE IS"BA
   CHR$(13)"DEGREES."
100 IF QA<90 AND AS<BS GOTO 110 EL
    SE END
110 PRINT"A SECOND SOLUTION EXISTS
    FOR THIS TRIANGLE."
120 BA=180-BA
130 CA=180-BA-AA*57.29578
140 CS=AS*SIN(CA*.01745329)/SIN(AA
    )
```

```
150 PRINT"FOR THE SECOND SOLUTION,
    THE THIRD SIDE IS"CS", ITS"CH
    R$(13)"ASSOCIATED ANGLE IS"CA"
    DEGREES AND THE FIRST SIDE'S"C
    HR$(13)"ASSOCIATED ANGLE IS"BA
```

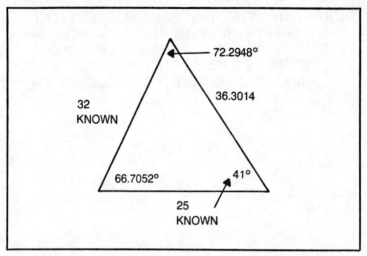

Fig. 5-13. A triangle with two known sides and a non-included angle.

Two Sides, Non-Included Angle Example

Using Fig. 5-13, solve for the unknown sides and angles.
ENTER THE TWO SIDES AND THE NON-INCLUDED ANGLE
ENTER FIRST SIDE, SECOND SIDE AND ITS ASSOCIATED ANGLE
? 35,25,41
THE THIRD SIDE IS 36.3014, ITS ASSOCIATED ANGLE IS 72.2948
DEGREES AND THE FIRST SIDE'S ASSOCIATED ANGLE IS 66.7052
DEGREES.
A SECOND SOLUTION EXISTS FOR THIS TRIANGLE.
FOR THE SECOND SOLUTION, THE THIRD SIDE IS 16.5283, ITS ASSOCIATED ANGLE IS 25.7052 DEGREES AND THE FIRST SIDE'S
ASSOCIATED ANGLE IS 113.295

This example illustrates that it is possible to have two solutions for this triangle. When using degrees, they must be in a decimal format, not minutes and seconds.

Three Sides Program

```
5 '3 SIDES
10 CLS
20 INPUT"ENTER THE THREE SIDES OF
   THE TRIANGLE";A,B,C
30 D=(A^2+B^2-C^2)/(2*A*B)
40 CA=-ATN(D/SQR(-D*D+1))+1.5708
50 Z=SIN(CA)/C
60 CA=CA*57.29578
70 BA=ATN((B*Z)/SQR(-B^2*Z*Z+1))
80 BA=BA*57.29578
90 AA=ATN((A*Z)/SQR(-A^2*Z*Z+1))
100 AA=AA*57.29578
110 PRINT"THE THREE CORRESPONDING
    ANGLES (A,B,C) ARE"CHR$(13)AA"
    DEGREES"CHR$(13)BA"DEGREES"CHR
    $(13)CA"DEGREES"
```

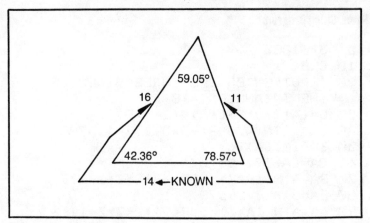

Fig. 5-14. A triangle with three sides, unknown angles.

Three Sides Example

In this example, the three sides are known, and you must determine the three included angles (use Fig. 5-14).
ENTER THE THREE SIDES OF THE TRIANGLE?
? 11, 14, 16
THE THREE CORRESPONDING ANGLES (A, B, C) ARE
42.3674 DEGREES
59.0558 DEGREES
78.5771 DEGREES

Two Angles and Opposite Side Program

```
5 '2 SIDES, OPPOSITE ANGLE
10 CLS
20 INPUT"ENTER THE TWO ANGLES (A,B
   ) AND THE OPPOSITE SIDE";AA,BA,
   CS
30 CA=180-AA-BA
40 BS=CS*SIN(BA/57.29578)/SIN(AA/5
   7.29578)
50 CS=CS*SIN(CA/57.29578)/SIN(AA/5
   7.29578)
60 PRINT"THE THIRD ANGLE IS"CA"DEG
   REES AND THE TWO UNKNOWN OPPOSI
   TE"CHR$(13)"SIDES ARE"BS"AND"CS
```

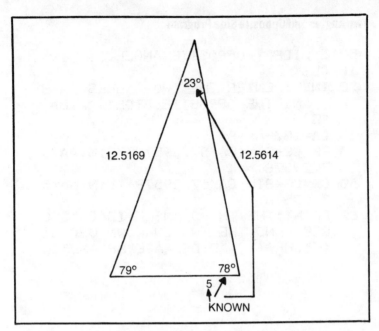

Fig. 5-15. A triangle with two known sides, opposite angles.

Two Angles and Opposite Side Example

Using Fig. 5-15, solve for the remaining angle and two sides.
ENTER THE TWO ANGLES (A,B) AND THE OPPOSITE SIDE?
? 23,78,5
THE THIRD ANGLE IS 79 DEGREES AND THE TWO UN-
KNOWN OPPOSITE SIDES ARE 12.5169 AND 12.5614.

Two Sides, Included Angle Program

```
5  '2 SIDES, INCLUDED ANGLE
10 CLS
20 INPUT"ENTER THE TWO SIDES (A,B)
   AND THE INCLUDED ANGLE";AS,BS,
   CA
30 CS=SQR(AS^2+BS^2-(2*AS*BS*COS(C
   A/57.29578)))
40 AA=ATN(AS*SIN(CA/57.29578)/CS/S
   QR(-AS*SIN(CA/57.29578)/CS*AS*S
   IN(CA/57.29578)/CS+1))
50 AA=AA*57.29578
60 BA=180-AA-CA
70 PRINT"THE THIRD SIDE IS"CS"."CH
   R$(13)"THE CORRESPONDING ANGLES
    FOR THE TWO KNOWN SIDES ARE"AA
   CHR$(13)"AND"BA"DEGREES."
```

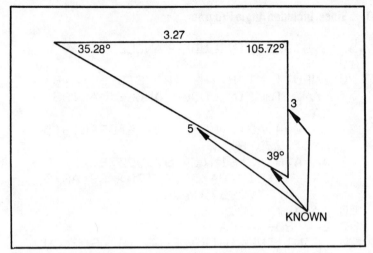

Fig. 5-16. A triangle with two known sides, included angle.

Two Sides, Included Angle Example

Solve Fig. 5-16 for the unknown side and angles.
ENTER THE TWO SIDES (A,B) AND THE INCLUDED ANG-
LE?
? 3,5,39
THE THIRD SIDE IS 3.26889.
THE CORRESPONDING ANGLES FOR THE TWO KNOWN
SIDES ARE 35.2787 AND 105.721 DEGREES.

GREAT CIRCLE CALCULATIONS

The last program in this chapter will compute the distance in nautical miles and bearing (referenced to True North) between two points on the Earth. Information for this program must be entered as decimal degrees. Plus, Southern Latitudes and Eastern Longitudes must be entered as negative numbers.

The equations to manually calculate the distance and bearing are:

$A = (\sin LA1 \cdot \sin LAZ + COS\ LA1 \cdot COS\ LAZ \cdot COS\ (LO2\text{-}LO1)$

$D = 60 \cdot Cos^{-1}A$

$$C = \frac{\sin LA2 - (\sin LA1 \cos D/60)}{\sin (D/60) \cos LA1}$$

$H = \cos^{-1}C$

Great Circle Program

```
5 'gREAT CIRCLE
10 CLS
20 PRINT"WHEN ENTERING DATA, SOUTHERN LATITUDES AND EASTERN
   LONGITUDES MUST BE ENTERED AS NEGATIVE NUMBERS."
25 PRINT
30 PRINT"ENTER LATITUDE AND LONGITUDE (1AT, 10N) OF THE
   STARTING POINT
40 INPUT LA(1),LO(1)
45 PRINT
50 PRINT"ENTER LATITUDE AND LONGITUDE (LAT,LON) OF THE
   DESTINATION"
55 INPUT LA(2),LO(2)
60 PRINT
70 A=SIN(LA(1)*.01745329)*SIN(LA(2)*.01745329)+COS(LA(1)*.01745
   329)*COS(LA(2)*.01745329)*COS((LO(2)-LO(1))*.01745329)
80 D=60*(-ATN(A/SQR(-A*A+1))+1.5708)*57.29579
90 C=(SIN(LA(2)*.01745329)-(SIN(LA(1)*.01745329)*COS(D/60*.0174
   5329)))/(SIN(D/60*.01745329)*COS(LA(1)*.01745329))
100 H=(-ATN(C/SQR(-C*C+1))+1.5708)*57.29579
110 F=SIN(LO(2)-LO(1))
120 IF F>=0 H=360-H
130 PRINT"tHE DISTANCE IS"D"NAUTICAL MILES AT A BEARING OF
    "H"DEGREES."
```

Great Circle Example

Compute the great circle distance and bearing from San Francisco to Tokoyo.

	Latitude	Longitude
San Francisco	37.82 N	122.42 W
Tokoyo	35.67 N	139.75 E

WHEN ENTERING DATA, SOUTHERN LATITUDES AND EASTERN LONGITUDES MUST BE ENTERED AS NEGATIVE NUMBERS.
ENTER LATITUDE AND LONGITUDE (LAT, LON) OF THE STARTING POINT
? 37.82, 122.42
ENTER LATITUDE AND LONGITUDE (LAT, LON) OF THE DESTINATION
? 35.67, – 139.75
THE DISTANCE IS 4456.89 NAUTICAL MILES AT A BEARING OF
303.292 DEGREES.

Again note that the Eastern Longitude of Tokoyo was entered as a negative number.

Appendix A
Statements and
Commands in BASIC

AUTO	turn on automatic line numbering. Can be set for different increments.
CLEAR	set numerics to zero, strings to null.
CLEAR N	same as CLEAR but sets aside a certain amount of memory for strings (N).
CLOAD	load program from cassette player. If no file-name is specified, the current program will be loaded.
CLOAD?	compares program on tape with program in memory. If programs are not equal "BAD" will be printed on video display.

CONT	continue after BREAK or STOP in execution.
CSAVE	saves current program on cassette tape, a file-name should be used so that program can be compared with what is in memory.
DATA	hold DATA for accessby READ statement.
DELETE	delete program line or lines specified by INPUT statement.
DIM	allocate storage for dimensional array with specified size per dimension.
EDIT	puts computer in EDIT mode for line specified.
END	end execution of program, returns computer to command mode.
ERROR	if an error is encountered in the program, the computer prints the offending line number and the error code for that line.
FOR—TO-	open a FOR-NEXT loop.
FOR—TO-STEP—	open a FOR-NEXT loop with optional STEP. If no step is specified an increment of one is used.
GOTO	branch to a specified line number in the program.

GOSUB	branch to a sub-routine beginning with the specified line number.
IF-THEN-ELSE	test expression; if true, execute the statement and jump to the next program line. If it's false, the ELSE statement will be executed.
INPUT	await input from keyboard.
INPUT #-1	input from cassette #1.
LET (var-exp)	assigns the value of an expression to variable. The LET is optional with LEVEL II BASIC.
LIST	list all program lines, or a specified range of lines.
NEXT var.	close the FOR - NEXT loop. The variable may be omitted, or a variable list may be used to close nested loops.
NEW	deletes the entire program in memory and returns to command mode.
ON-GOTO	branches to a specified line number after evaluating the expression. Otherwise go to the next statement.
ON-GOSUB	same as ON - GOTO but branches to the appropriate

	GOSUB statement.
PRINT exp.	outputs to the video display the value of exp, which can be a string expression, a numeric, a constant or a list of items.
PRINT #-1	output to cassette #1
PRINT	begins printing at a specified area on the video display; a PRINT modifier.
PRINT USING	PRINT format specifier, output exp in a form specified by a string field.
RANDOM	reseeds the RANDOM number generator.
REM	remark indicator. The rest of line is ignored.
READ	assigns values to specified variables starting with the current DATA element.
RESTORE	resets the data pointer to the first item in the first DATA statement.
RESUME	returns from the error routine to the line specified.
RETURN	branch statement *following* last GOSUB executed.
RUN	execute the program. If no line is specified, execution begins with the program's lowest line number.
STOP	stop the program's exe-

	cution and print a break message containing current line number. Program execution can resume with CONT.
SYSTEM	enter the monitor code for loading a machine language program from cassette tape player.
TAB	print modifier; begins printing at specified TAB area of the video display.
TROFF	turn off the line-numbers trace.
TRON	turn on the line numbers trace (very useful when debugging).

String Functions

ASC	returns the ASCII code of first character in string argument.
CHR$	returns a one-character string defined by a code. If a contol function is specified by code, that function is acti-vated.
FRE	returns amount of memory available for string storage.
INKEY$	strobes the keyboard and

	returns a one-character string corresponding to the key pressed during strobe.
LEN	returns the numeric length of string.
LEFT$	returns the first n characters of a string (when n is a numeric expression).
MID$	returns the substring of a string with length n and starting at position
MID$ (cont)	m in a string (where n and m are numeric expressions).
RIGHT$	returns the last n characters of a string (where n is a numeric expression).
STR$	returns a string representation of an evaluated argument.
STRING$	returns a sequence of characters using the first character. PRINT STRINGS$ (50, "*"), for example, will print 50 asterisks on the video display.
VAL	returns a numeric value corresponding to a numeric-valued string, such as PRINT VAL (A$+W$).

Appendix B
Powers of Two

n	2^n	2^n THREE BYTE BINARY		
0	1	00000000	00000000	00000001
1	2	00000000	00000000	00000010
2	4	00000000	00000000	00000100
3	8	00000000	00000000	00001000
4	16	00000000	00000000	00010000
5	32	00000000	00000000	00100000
6	64	00000000	00000000	01000000
7	128	00000000	00000000	10000000
8	256	00000000	00000001	00000000
9	512	00000000	00000010	00000000
10	1024	00000000	00000100	00000000
11	2048	00000000	00001000	00000000
12	4096	00000000	00010000	00000000
13	8192	00000000	00100000	00000000
14	16384	00000000	01000000	00000000
15	32768	00000000	10000000	00000000
16	65536	00000001	00000000	00000000
17	131072	00000010	00000000	00000000
18	262144	00000100	00000000	00000000
19	524288	00001000	00000000	00000000
20	1048576	00010000	00000000	00000000
21	2097152	00100000	00000000	00000000
22	4194304	01000000	00000000	00000000
23	8388608	10000000	00000000	00000000

Appendix C
Hexadecimal-Decimal Integer Conversion

The following table provides for direct conversions between hexadecimal integers in the range 0–FFF and decimal integers in the range 0–4095. For conversion of larger integers, the table values may be added to the following figures:

Hexadecimal	Decimal	Hexadecimal	Decimal
01 000	4 096	20 000	131 072
02 000	8 192	30 000	196 608
03 000	12 288	40 000	262 144
04 000	16 384	50 000	327 680
05 000	20 480	60 000	393 216
06 000	24 576	70 000	458 752
07 000	28 672	80 000	524 288
08 000	32 768	90 000	589 824
09 000	36 864	A0 000	655 360
0A 000	40 960	B0 000	720 896
0B 000	45 056	C0 000	786 432
0C 000	49 152	D0 000	851 968
0D 000	53 248	E0 000	917 504
0E 000	57 344	F0 000	983 040
0F 000	61 440	100 000	1 048 576
10 000	65 536	200 000	2 097 152
11 000	69 632	300 000	3 145 728
12 000	73 728	400 000	4 194 304
13 000	77 824	500 000	5 242 880
14 000	81 920	600 000	6 291 456
15 000	86 016	700 000	7 340 032
16 000	90 112	800 000	8 388 608
17 000	94 208	900 000	9 437 184
18 000	98 304	A00 000	10 485 760
19 000	102 400	B00 000	11 534 336
1A 000	106 496	C00 000	12 582 912
1B 000	110 592	D00 000	13 631 488
1C 000	114 688	E00 000	14 680 064
1D 000	118 784	F00 000	15 728 640
1E 000	122 880	1 000 000	16 777 216
1F 000	126 976	2 000 000	33 554 432

HEXADECIMAL-DECIMAL INTEGER CONVERSION

	0	1	2	3	4	5	6	7	8	9	A	B	C	D	E	F
000	0000	0001	0002	0003	0004	0005	0006	0007	0008	0009	0010	0011	0012	0013	0014	0015
010	0016	0017	0018	0019	0020	0021	0022	0023	0024	0025	0026	0027	0028	0029	0030	0031
020	0032	0033	0034	0035	0036	0037	0038	0039	0040	0041	0042	0043	0044	0045	0046	0047
030	0048	0049	0050	0051	0052	0053	0054	0055	0056	0057	0058	0059	0060	0061	0062	0063
040	0064	0065	0066	0067	0068	0069	0070	0071	0072	0073	0074	0075	0076	0077	0078	0079
050	0080	0081	0082	0083	0084	0085	0086	0087	0088	0089	0090	0091	0092	0093	0094	0095
060	0096	0097	0098	0099	0100	0101	0102	0103	0104	0105	0106	0107	0108	0109	0110	0111
070	0112	0113	0114	0115	0116	0117	0118	0119	0120	0121	0122	0123	0124	0125	0126	0127
080	0128	0129	0130	0131	0132	0133	0134	0135	0136	0137	0138	0139	0140	0141	0142	0143
090	0144	0145	0146	0147	0148	0149	0150	0151	0152	0153	0154	0155	0156	0157	0158	0159
0A0	0160	0161	0162	0163	0164	0165	0166	0167	0168	0169	0170	0171	0172	0173	0174	0175
0B0	0176	0177	0178	0179	0180	0181	0182	0183	0184	0185	0186	0187	0188	0189	0190	0191
0C0	0192	0193	0194	0195	0196	0197	0198	0199	0200	0201	0202	0203	0204	0205	0206	0207
0D0	0208	0209	0210	0211	0212	0213	0214	0215	0216	0217	0218	0219	0220	0221	0222	0223
0E0	0224	0225	0226	0227	0228	0229	0230	0231	0232	0233	0234	0235	0236	0237	0238	0239
0F0	0240	0241	0242	0243	0244	0245	0246	0247	0248	0249	0250	0251	0252	0253	0254	0255

Hex	0	1	2	3	4	5	6	7	8	9	A	B	C	D	E	F
100	0256	0257	0258	0259	0260	0261	0262	0263	0264	0265	0266	0267	0268	0269	0270	0271
110	0272	0273	0274	0275	0276	0277	0278	0279	0280	0281	0282	0283	0284	0285	0286	0287
120	0288	0289	0290	0291	0292	0293	0294	0295	0296	0297	0298	0299	0300	0301	0302	0303
130	0304	0305	0306	0307	0308	0309	0310	0311	0312	0313	0314	0315	0316	0317	0318	0319
140	0320	0321	0322	0323	0324	0325	0326	0327	0328	0329	0330	0331	0332	0333	0334	0335
150	0336	0337	0338	0339	0340	0341	0342	0343	0344	0345	0346	0347	0348	0349	0350	0351
160	0352	0353	0354	0355	0356	0357	0358	0359	0360	0361	0362	0363	0364	0365	0366	0367
170	0368	0369	0370	0371	0372	0373	0374	0375	0376	0377	0378	0379	0380	0381	0382	0383
180	0384	0385	0386	0387	0388	0389	0390	0391	0392	0393	0394	0395	0396	0397	0398	0399
190	0400	0401	0402	0403	0404	0405	0406	0407	0408	0409	0410	0411	0412	0413	0414	0415
1A0	0416	0417	0418	0419	0420	0421	0422	0423	0424	0425	0426	0427	0428	0429	0430	0431
1B0	0432	0433	0434	0435	0436	0437	0438	0439	0440	0441	0442	0443	0444	0445	0446	0447
1C0	0448	0449	0450	0451	0452	0453	0454	0455	0456	0457	0458	0459	0460	0461	0462	0463
1D0	0464	0465	0466	0467	0468	0469	0470	0471	0472	0473	0474	0475	0476	0477	0478	0479
1E0	0480	0481	0482	0483	0484	0485	0486	0487	0488	0489	0490	0491	0492	0493	0494	0495
1F0	0496	0497	0498	0499	0500	0501	0502	0503	0504	0505	0506	0507	0508	0509	0510	0511
200	0512	0513	0514	0515	0516	0517	0518	0519	0520	0521	0522	0523	0524	0525	0526	0527
210	0528	0529	0530	0531	0532	0533	0534	0535	0536	0537	0538	0539	0540	0541	0542	0543
220	0544	0545	0546	0547	0548	0549	0550	0551	0552	0553	0554	0555	0556	0557	0558	0559
230	0560	0561	0562	0563	0564	0565	0566	0567	0568	0569	0570	0571	0572	0573	0574	0575
240	0576	0577	0578	0579	0580	0581	0582	0583	0584	0585	0586	0587	0588	0589	0590	0591
250	0592	0593	0594	0595	0596	0597	0598	0599	0600	0601	0602	0603	0604	0605	0606	0607
260	0608	0609	0610	0611	0612	0613	0614	0615	0616	0617	0618	0619	0620	0621	0622	0623
270	0624	0625	0626	0627	0628	0629	0630	0631	0632	0633	0634	0635	0636	0637	0638	0639

HEXADECIMAL-DECIMAL INTEGER CONVERSION (continued)

	0	1	2	3	4	5	6	7	8	9	A	B	C	D	E	F
280	0640	0641	0642	0643	0644	0645	0646	0647	0648	0649	0650	0651	0652	0653	0654	0655
290	0656	0657	0658	0659	0660	0661	0662	0663	0664	0665	0666	0667	0668	0669	0670	0671
2A0	0672	0673	0674	0675	0676	0677	0678	0679	0680	0681	0682	0683	0684	0685	0686	0687
2B0	0688	0689	0690	0691	0692	0693	0694	0695	0696	0697	0698	0699	0700	0701	0702	0703
2C0	0704	0705	0706	0707	0708	0709	0710	0711	0712	0713	0714	0715	0716	0717	0718	0719
2D0	0720	0721	0722	0723	0724	0725	0726	0727	0728	0729	0730	0731	0732	0733	0734	0735
2E0	0736	0737	0738	0739	0740	0741	0742	0743	0744	0745	0746	0747	0748	0749	0750	0751
2F0	0752	0753	0754	0755	0756	0757	0758	0759	0760	0761	0762	0763	0764	0765	0766	0767
300	0768	0769	0770	0771	0772	0773	0774	0775	0776	0777	0778	0779	0780	0781	0782	0783
310	0784	0785	0786	0787	0788	0789	0790	0791	0792	0793	0794	0795	0796	0797	0798	0799
320	0800	0801	0802	0803	0804	0805	0806	0807	0808	0809	0810	0811	0812	0813	0814	0815
330	0816	0817	0818	0819	0820	0821	0822	0823	0824	0825	0826	0827	0828	0829	0830	0831
340	0832	0833	0834	0835	0836	0837	0838	0839	0840	0841	0842	0843	0844	0845	0846	0847
350	0848	0849	0850	0851	0852	0853	0854	0855	0856	0857	0858	0859	0860	0861	0862	0863
360	0864	0865	0866	0867	0868	0869	0870	0871	0872	0873	0874	0875	0876	0877	0878	0879
370	0880	0881	0882	0883	0884	0885	0886	0887	0888	0889	0890	0891	0892	0893	0894	0895
380	0896	0897	0898	0899	0900	0901	0902	0903	0904	0905	0906	0907	0908	0909	0910	0911
390	0912	0913	0914	0915	0916	0917	0918	0919	0920	0921	0922	0923	0924	0925	0926	0927
3A0	0928	0929	0930	0931	0932	0933	0934	0935	0936	0937	0938	0939	0940	0941	0942	0943
3B0	0944	0945	0946	0947	0948	0949	0950	0951	0952	0953	0954	0955	0956	0957	0958	0959
3C0	0960	0961	0962	0963	0964	0965	0966	0967	0968	0969	0970	0971	0972	0973	0974	0975
3D0	0976	0977	0978	0979	0980	0981	0982	0983	0984	0985	0986	0987	0988	0989	0990	0991
3E0	0992	0993	0994	0995	0996	0997	0998	0999	1000	1001	1002	1003	1004	1005	1006	1007
3F0	1008	1009	1010	1011	1012	1013	1014	1015	1016	1017	1018	1019	1020	1021	1022	1023

Hex																
400	1039	1038	1037	1036	1035	1034	1033	1032	1031	1030	1029	1028	1027	1026	1025	1024
410	1055	1054	1053	1052	1051	1050	1049	1048	1047	1046	1045	1044	1043	1042	1041	1040
420	1071	1070	1069	1068	1067	1066	1065	1064	1063	1062	1061	1060	1059	1058	1057	1056
430	1087	1086	1085	1084	1083	1082	1081	1080	1079	1078	1077	1076	1075	1074	1073	1072
440	1103	1102	1101	1100	1099	1098	1097	1096	1095	1094	1093	1092	1091	1090	1089	1088
450	1119	1118	1117	1116	1115	1114	1113	1112	1111	1110	1109	1108	1107	1106	1105	1104
460	1135	1134	1133	1132	1131	1130	1129	1128	1127	1126	1125	1124	1123	1122	1121	1120
470	1151	1150	1149	1148	1147	1146	1145	1144	1143	1142	1141	1140	1139	1138	1137	1136
480	1167	1166	1165	1164	1163	1162	1161	1160	1159	1158	1157	1156	1155	1154	1153	1152
490	1183	1182	1181	1180	1179	1178	1177	1176	1175	1174	1173	1172	1171	1170	1169	1168
4A0	1199	1198	1197	1196	1195	1194	1193	1192	1191	1190	1189	1188	1187	1186	1185	1184
4B0	1215	1214	1213	1212	1211	1210	1209	1208	1207	1206	1205	1204	1203	1202	1201	1200
4C0	1231	1230	1229	1228	1227	1226	1225	1224	1223	1222	1221	1220	1219	1218	1217	1216
4D0	1247	1246	1245	1244	1243	1242	1241	1240	1239	1238	1237	1236	1235	1234	1233	1232
4E0	1263	1262	1261	1260	1259	1258	1257	1256	1255	1254	1253	1252	1251	1250	1249	1248
4F0	1279	1278	1277	1276	1275	1274	1273	1272	1271	1270	1269	1268	1267	1266	1265	1264
500	1295	1294	1293	1292	1291	1290	1289	1288	1287	1286	1285	1284	1283	1282	1281	1280
510	1311	1310	1309	1308	1307	1306	1305	1304	1303	1302	1301	1300	1299	1298	1297	1296
520	1327	1326	1325	1324	1323	1322	1321	1320	1319	1318	1317	1316	1315	1314	1313	1312
530	1343	1342	1341	1340	1339	1338	1337	1336	1335	1334	1333	1332	1331	1330	1329	1328
540	1359	1358	1357	1356	1355	1354	1353	1352	1351	1350	1349	1348	1347	1346	1345	1344
550	1375	1374	1373	1372	1371	1370	1369	1368	1367	1366	1365	1364	1363	1362	1361	1360
560	1391	1390	1389	1388	1387	1386	1385	1384	1383	1382	1381	1380	1379	1378	1377	1376
570	1407	1406	1405	1404	1403	1402	1401	1400	1399	1398	1397	1396	1395	1394	1393	1392

	0	1	2	3	4	5	6	7	8	9	A	B	C	D	E	F
580	1408	1409	1410	1411	1412	1413	1414	1415	1416	1417	1418	1419	1420	1421	1422	1423
590	1424	1425	1426	1427	1428	1429	1430	1431	1432	1433	1434	1435	1436	1437	1438	1439
5A0	1440	1441	1442	1443	1444	1445	1446	1447	1448	1449	1450	1451	1452	1453	1454	1455
5B0	1456	1457	1458	1459	1460	1461	1462	1463	1464	1465	1466	1467	1468	1469	1470	1471
5C0	1472	1473	1474	1475	1476	1477	1478	1479	1480	1481	1482	1483	1484	1485	1486	1487
5D0	1488	1489	1490	1491	1492	1493	1494	1495	1496	1497	1498	1499	1500	1501	1502	1503
5E0	1504	1505	1506	1507	1508	1509	1510	1511	1512	1513	1514	1515	1516	1517	1518	1519
5F0	1520	1521	1522	1523	1524	1525	1526	1527	1528	1529	1530	1531	1532	1533	1534	1535
600	1536	1537	1538	1539	1540	1541	1542	1543	1544	1545	1546	1547	1548	1549	1550	1551
610	1552	1553	1554	1555	1556	1557	1558	1559	1560	1561	1562	1563	1564	1565	1566	1567
620	1568	1569	1570	1571	1572	1573	1574	1575	1576	1577	1578	1579	1580	1581	1582	1583
630	1584	1585	1586	1587	1588	1589	1590	1591	1592	1593	1594	1595	1596	1597	1598	1599
640	1600	1601	1602	1603	1604	1605	1606	1607	1608	1609	1610	1611	1612	1613	1614	1615
650	1616	1617	1618	1619	1620	1621	1622	1623	1624	1625	1626	1627	1628	1629	1630	1631
660	1632	1633	1634	1635	1636	1637	1638	1639	1640	1641	1642	1643	1644	1645	1646	1647
670	1648	1649	1650	1651	1652	1653	1654	1655	1656	1657	1658	1659	1660	1661	1662	1663
680	1664	1665	1666	1667	1668	1669	1670	1671	1672	1673	1674	1675	1676	1677	1678	1679
690	1680	1681	1682	1683	1684	1685	1686	1687	1688	1689	1690	1691	1692	1693	1694	1695
6A0	1696	1697	1698	1699	1700	1701	1702	1703	1704	1705	1706	1707	1708	1709	1710	1711
6B0	1712	1713	1714	1715	1716	1717	1718	1719	1720	1721	1722	1723	1724	1725	1726	1727
6C0	1728	1729	1730	1731	1732	1733	1734	1735	1736	1737	1738	1739	1740	1741	1742	1743
6D0	1744	1745	1746	1747	1748	1749	1750	1751	1752	1753	1754	1755	1756	1757	1758	1759
6E0	1760	1761	1762	1763	1764	1765	1766	1767	1768	1769	1770	1771	1772	1773	1774	1775
6F0	1776	1777	1778	1779	1780	1781	1782	1783	1784	1785	1786	1787	1788	1789	1790	1791

	0	1	2	3	4	5	6	7	8	9	A	B	C	D	E	F
700	1792	1793	1794	1795	1796	1797	1798	1799	1800	1801	1802	1803	1804	1805	1806	1807
710	1808	1809	1810	1811	1812	1813	1814	1815	1816	1817	1818	1819	1820	1821	1822	1823
720	1824	1825	1826	1827	1828	1829	1830	1831	1832	1833	1834	1835	1836	1837	1838	1839
730	1840	1841	1842	1843	1844	1845	1846	1847	1848	1849	1850	1851	1852	1853	1854	1855
740	1856	1857	1858	1859	1860	1861	1862	1863	1864	1865	1866	1867	1868	1869	1870	1871
750	1872	1873	1874	1875	1876	1877	1878	1879	1880	1881	1882	1883	1884	1885	1886	1887
760	1888	1889	1890	1891	1892	1893	1894	1895	1896	1897	1898	1899	1900	1901	1902	1903
770	1904	1905	1906	1907	1908	1909	1910	1911	1912	1913	1914	1915	1916	1917	1918	1919
780	1920	1921	1922	1923	1924	1925	1926	1927	1928	1929	1930	1931	1932	1933	1934	1935
790	1936	1937	1938	1939	1940	1941	1942	1943	1944	1945	1946	1947	1948	1949	1950	1951
7A0	1952	1953	1954	1955	1956	1957	1958	1959	1960	1961	1962	1963	1964	1965	1966	1967
7B0	1968	1969	1970	1971	1972	1973	1974	1975	1976	1977	1978	1979	1980	1981	1982	1983
7C0	1984	1985	1986	1987	1988	1989	1990	1991	1992	1993	1994	1995	1996	1997	1998	1999
7D0	2000	2001	2002	2003	2004	2005	2006	2007	2008	2009	2010	2011	2012	2013	2014	2015
7E0	2016	2017	2018	2019	2020	2021	2022	2023	2024	2025	2026	2027	2028	2029	2030	2031
7F0	2032	2033	2034	2035	2036	2037	2038	2039	2040	2041	2042	2043	2044	2045	2046	2047
800	2048	2049	2050	2051	2052	2053	2054	2055	2056	2057	2058	2059	2060	2061	2062	2063
810	2064	2065	2066	2067	2068	2069	2070	2071	2072	2073	2074	2075	2076	2077	2078	2079
820	2080	2081	2082	2083	2084	2085	2086	2087	2088	2089	2090	2091	2092	2093	2094	2095
830	2096	2097	2098	2099	2100	2101	2102	2103	2104	2105	2106	2107	2108	2109	2110	2111
840	2112	2113	2114	2115	2116	2117	2118	2119	2120	2121	2122	2123	2124	2125	2126	2127
850	2128	2129	2130	2131	2132	2133	2134	2135	2136	2137	2138	2139	2140	2141	2142	2143
860	2144	2145	2146	2147	2148	2149	2150	2151	2152	2153	2154	2155	2156	2157	2158	2159
870	2160	2161	2162	2163	2164	2165	2166	2167	2168	2169	2170	2171	2172	2173	2174	2175

HEXADECIMAL-DECIMAL INTEGER CONVERSION (continued)

	0	1	2	3	4	5	6	7	8	9	A	B	C	D	E	F
880	2176	2177	2178	2179	2180	2181	2182	2183	2184	2185	2186	2187	2188	2189	2190	2191
890	2192	2193	2194	2195	2196	2197	2198	2199	2200	2201	2202	2203	2204	2205	2206	2207
8A0	2208	2209	2210	2211	2212	2213	2214	2215	2216	2217	2218	2219	2220	2221	2222	2223
8B0	2224	2225	2226	2227	2228	2229	2230	2231	2232	2233	2234	2235	2236	2237	2238	2239
8C0	2240	2241	2242	2243	2244	2245	2246	2247	2248	2249	2250	2251	2252	2253	2254	2255
8D0	2256	2257	2258	2259	2260	2261	2262	2263	2264	2265	2266	2267	2268	2269	2270	2271
8E0	2272	2273	2274	2275	2276	2277	2278	2279	2280	2281	2282	2283	2284	2285	2286	2287
8F0	2288	2289	2290	2291	2292	2293	2294	2295	2296	2297	2298	2299	2300	2301	2302	2303
900	2304	2305	2306	2307	2308	2309	2310	2311	2312	2313	2314	2315	2316	2317	2318	2319
910	2320	2321	2322	2323	2324	2325	2326	2327	2328	2329	2330	2331	2332	2333	2334	2335
920	2336	2337	2338	2339	2340	2341	2342	2343	2344	2345	2346	2347	2348	2349	2350	2351
930	2352	2353	2354	2355	2356	2357	2358	2359	2360	2361	2362	2363	2364	2365	2366	2367
940	2368	2369	2370	2371	2372	2373	2374	2375	2376	2377	2378	2379	2380	2381	2382	2383
950	2384	2385	2386	2387	2388	2389	2390	2391	2392	2393	2394	2395	2396	2397	2398	2399
960	2400	2401	2402	2403	2404	2405	2406	2407	2408	2409	2410	2411	2412	2413	2414	2415
970	2416	2417	2418	2419	2420	2421	2422	2423	2424	2425	2426	2427	2428	2429	2430	2431
980	2432	2433	2434	2435	2436	2437	2438	2439	2440	2441	2442	2443	2444	2445	2446	2447
990	2448	2449	2450	2451	2452	2453	2454	2455	2456	2457	2458	2459	2460	2461	2462	2463
9A0	2464	2465	2466	2467	2468	2469	2470	2471	2472	2473	2474	2475	2476	2477	2478	2479
9B0	2480	2481	2482	2483	2484	2485	2486	2487	2488	2489	2490	2491	2492	2493	2494	2495
9C0	2496	2497	2498	2499	2500	2501	2502	2503	2504	2505	2506	2507	2508	2509	2510	2511
9D0	2512	2513	2514	2515	2516	2517	2518	2519	2520	2521	2522	2523	2524	2525	2526	2527
9E0	2528	2529	2530	2531	2532	2533	2534	2535	2536	2537	2538	2539	2540	2541	2542	2543
9F0	2544	2545	2546	2547	2548	2549	2550	2551	2552	2553	2554	2555	2556	2557	2558	2559

	0	1	2	3	4	5	6	7	8	9	A	B	C	D	E	F
A00	2560	2561	2562	2563	2564	2565	2566	2567	2568	2569	2570	2571	2572	2573	2574	2575
A10	2576	2577	2578	2579	2580	2581	2582	2583	2584	2585	2586	2587	2588	2589	2590	2591
A20	2592	2593	2594	2595	2596	2597	2598	2599	2600	2601	2602	2603	2604	2605	2606	2607
A30	2608	2609	2610	2611	2612	2613	2614	2615	2616	2617	2618	2619	2620	2621	2622	2623
A40	2624	2625	2626	2627	2628	2629	2630	2631	2632	2633	2634	2635	2636	2637	2638	2639
A50	2640	2641	2642	2643	2644	2645	2646	2647	2648	2649	2650	2651	2652	2653	2654	2655
A60	2656	2657	2658	2659	2660	2661	2662	2663	2664	2665	2666	2667	2668	2669	2670	2671
A70	2672	2673	2674	2675	2676	2677	2678	2679	2680	2681	2682	2683	2684	2685	2686	2687
A80	2688	2689	2690	2691	2692	2693	2694	2695	2696	2697	2698	2699	2700	2701	2702	2703
A90	2704	2705	2706	2707	2708	2709	2710	2711	2712	2713	2714	2715	2716	2717	2718	2719
AA0	2720	2721	2722	2723	2724	2725	2726	2727	2728	2729	2730	2731	2732	2733	2734	2735
AB0	2736	2737	2738	2739	2740	2741	2742	2743	2744	2745	2746	2747	2748	2749	2750	2751
AC0	2752	2753	2754	2755	2756	2757	2758	2759	2760	2761	2762	2763	2764	2765	2766	2767
AD0	2768	2769	2770	2771	2772	2773	2774	2775	2776	2777	2778	2779	2780	2781	2782	2783
AE0	2784	2785	2786	2787	2788	2789	2790	2791	2792	2793	2794	2795	2796	2797	2793	2799
AF0	2800	2801	2802	2803	2804	2805	2806	2807	2808	2809	2810	2811	2812	2813	2814	2815
B00	2816	2817	2818	2819	2820	2821	2822	2823	2824	2825	2826	2827	2828	2829	2830	2831
B10	2832	2833	2834	2835	2836	2837	2838	2839	2840	2841	2842	2843	2844	2845	2846	2847
B20	2848	2849	2850	2851	2852	2853	2854	2855	2856	2857	2858	2859	2860	2861	2862	2863
B30	2864	2865	2866	2867	2868	2869	2870	2871	2872	2873	2874	2875	2876	2877	2878	2879
B40	2880	2881	2882	2883	2884	2885	2886	2887	2888	2889	2890	2891	2892	2893	2894	2895
B50	2896	2897	2898	2899	2900	2901	2902	2903	2904	2905	2906	2907	2908	2909	2910	2911
B60	2912	2913	2914	2915	2916	2917	2918	2919	2920	2921	2922	2923	2924	2925	2926	2927
B70	2928	2929	2930	2931	2932	2933	2934	2935	2936	2937	2938	2939	2940	2941	2942	2943

HEXADECIMAL-DECIMAL INTEGER CONVERSION (continued)

	0	1	2	3	4	5	6	7	8	9	A	B	C	D	E	F
B80	2944	2945	2946	2947	2948	2949	2950	2951	2952	2953	2954	2955	2956	2957	2958	2959
B90	2960	2961	2962	2963	2964	2965	2966	2967	2968	2969	2970	2971	2972	2973	2974	2975
BA0	2976	2977	2978	2979	2980	2981	2982	2983	2984	2985	2986	2987	2988	2989	2990	2991
BB0	2992	2993	2994	2995	2996	2997	2998	2999	3000	3001	3002	3003	3004	3005	3006	3007
BC0	3008	3009	3010	3011	3012	3013	3014	3015	3016	3017	3018	3019	3020	3021	3022	3023
BD0	3024	3025	3026	3027	3028	3029	3030	3031	3032	3033	3034	3035	3036	3037	3038	3039
BE0	3040	3041	3042	3043	3044	3045	3046	3047	3048	3049	3050	3051	3052	3053	3054	3055
BF0	3056	3057	3058	3059	3060	3061	3062	3063	3064	3065	3066	3067	3068	3069	3070	3071
C00	3072	3073	3074	3075	3076	3077	3078	3079	3080	3081	3082	3083	3084	3085	3086	3087
C10	3088	3089	3090	3091	3092	3093	3094	3095	3096	3097	3098	3099	3100	3101	3102	3103
C20	3104	3105	3106	3107	3108	3109	3110	3111	3112	3113	3114	3115	3116	3117	3118	3119
C30	3120	3121	3122	3123	3124	3125	3126	3127	3128	3129	3130	3131	3132	3133	3134	3135
C40	3136	3137	3138	3139	3140	3141	3142	3143	3144	3145	3146	3147	3148	3149	3150	3151
C50	3152	3153	3154	3155	3156	3157	3158	3159	3160	3161	3162	3163	3164	3165	3166	3167
C60	3168	3169	3170	3171	3172	3173	3174	3175	3176	3177	3178	3179	3180	3181	3182	3183
C70	3184	3185	3186	3187	3188	3189	3190	3191	3192	3193	3194	3195	3196	3197	3198	3199
C80	3200	3201	3202	3203	3204	3205	3206	3207	3208	3209	3210	3211	3212	3213	3214	3215
C90	3216	3217	3218	3219	3220	3221	3222	3223	3224	3225	3226	3227	3228	3229	3230	3231
CA0	3232	3233	3234	3235	3236	3237	3238	3239	3240	3241	3242	3243	3244	3245	3246	3247
CB0	3248	3249	3250	3251	3252	3253	3254	3255	3256	3257	3258	3259	3260	3261	3262	3263
CC0	3264	3265	3266	3267	3268	3269	3270	3271	3272	3273	3274	3275	3276	3277	3278	3279
CD0	3280	3281	3282	3283	3284	3285	3286	3287	3288	3289	3290	3291	3292	3293	3294	3295
CE0	3296	3297	3298	3299	3300	3301	3302	3303	3304	3305	3306	3307	3308	3309	3310	3311
CF0	3312	3313	3314	3315	3316	3317	3318	3319	3320	3321	3322	3323	3324	3325	3326	3327

	0	1	2	3	4	5	6	7	8	9	A	B	C	D	E	F
D00	3328	3329	3330	3331	3332	3333	3334	3335	3336	3337	3338	3339	3340	3341	3342	3343
D10	3344	3345	3346	3347	3348	3349	3350	3351	3352	3353	3354	3355	3356	3357	3358	3359
D20	3360	3361	3362	3363	3364	3365	3366	3367	3368	3369	3370	3371	3372	3373	3374	3375
D30	3376	3377	3378	3379	3380	3381	3382	3383	3384	3385	3386	3387	3388	3389	3390	3391
D40	3392	3393	3394	3395	3396	3397	3398	3399	3400	3401	3402	3403	3404	3405	3406	3407
D50	3408	3409	3410	3411	3412	3413	3414	3415	3416	3417	3418	3419	3420	3421	3422	3423
D60	3424	3425	3426	3427	3428	3429	3430	3431	3432	3433	3434	3435	3436	3437	3438	3439
D70	3440	3441	3442	3443	3444	3445	3446	3447	3448	3449	3450	3451	3452	3453	3454	3455
D80	3456	3457	3458	3459	3460	3461	3462	3463	3464	3465	3466	3467	3468	3469	3470	3471
D90	3472	3473	3474	3475	3476	3477	3478	3479	3480	3481	3482	3483	3484	3485	3486	3487
DA0	3488	3489	3490	3491	3492	3493	3494	3495	3496	3497	3498	3499	3500	3501	3502	3503
DB0	3504	3505	3506	3507	3508	3509	3510	3511	3512	3513	3514	3515	3516	3517	3518	3519
DC0	3520	3521	3522	3523	3524	3525	3526	3527	3528	3529	3530	3531	3532	3533	3534	3535
DD0	3536	3537	3538	3539	3540	3541	3542	3543	3544	3545	3546	3547	3548	3549	3550	3551
DE0	3552	3553	3554	3555	3556	3557	3558	3559	3560	3561	3562	3563	3564	3565	3566	3567
DF0	3568	3569	3570	3571	3572	3573	3574	3575	3576	3577	3578	3579	3580	3581	3582	3583
E00	3584	3585	3586	3587	3588	3589	3590	3591	3592	3593	3594	3595	3596	3597	3598	3599
E10	3600	3601	3602	3603	3604	3605	3606	3607	3608	3609	3610	3611	3612	3613	3614	3615
E20	3616	3617	3618	3619	3620	3621	3622	3623	3624	3625	3626	3627	3628	3629	3630	3631
E30	3632	3633	3634	3635	3636	3637	3638	3639	3640	3641	3642	3643	3644	3645	3646	3647
E40	3648	3649	3650	3651	3652	3653	3654	3655	3656	3657	3658	3659	3660	3661	3662	3663
E50	3664	3665	3666	3667	3668	3669	3670	3671	3672	3673	3674	3675	3676	3677	3678	3679
E60	3680	3681	3682	3683	3684	3685	3686	3687	3688	3689	3690	3691	3692	3693	3694	3695
E70	3696	3697	3698	3699	3700	3701	3702	3703	3704	3705	3706	3707	3708	3709	3710	3711

HEXADECIMAL-DECIMAL INTEGER CONVERSION (continued)

	0	1	2	3	4	5	6	7	8	9	A	B	C	D	E	F
E80	3712	3713	3714	1715	3716	3717	3718	3719	3720	3721	3722	3723	3724	3725	3726	3727
E90	3728	3729	3730	3731	3732	3733	3734	3735	3736	3737	3738	3739	3740	3741	3742	3743
EA0	3744	3745	3746	3747	3748	3749	3750	3751	3752	3753	3754	3755	3756	3757	3758	3759
EB0	3760	3761	3762	3763	3764	3765	3766	3767	3768	3769	3770	3771	3772	3773	3774	3775
EC0	3776	3777	3778	3779	3780	3781	3782	3783	3784	3785	3786	3787	3788	3789	3790	3791
ED0	3792	3793	3794	3795	3796	3797	3798	3799	3800	3801	3802	3803	3804	3805	3806	3807
EE0	3808	3809	3810	3811	3812	3813	3814	3815	3816	3817	3818	3819	3820	3821	3822	3823
EF0	3824	3825	3826	3827	3828	3829	3830	3831	3832	3833	3834	3835	3836	3837	3838	3839
F00	3840	3841	3842	3843	3844	3845	3846	3847	3848	3849	3850	3851	3852	3853	3854	3855
F10	3856	3857	3858	3859	3860	3861	3862	3863	3864	3865	3866	3867	3868	3869	3870	3871
F20	3872	3873	3874	3875	3876	3877	3878	3879	3880	3881	3882	3883	3884	3885	3886	3887
F30	3888	3889	3890	3891	3892	3893	3894	3895	3896	3897	3898	3899	3900	3901	3902	3903
F40	3904	3905	3906	3907	3908	3909	3910	3911	3912	2313	3914	3915	3916	3917	3918	3919
F50	3920	3921	3922	3923	3924	2925	3926	3927	3928	3929	3930	3931	3932	3933	3934	3935
F60	3936	3937	3938	3939	3940	3941	3942	3943	3944	3945	394	3947	3948	3949	3950	3951
F70	3952	3953	3954	3955	3956	3957	3958	3959	3960	3961	3962	3963	3964	3965	3966	3967
F8C	3968	3969	3970	3971	3972	3973	3974	3975	3976	3977	3978	3979	3980	3981	3982	3983
F90	3984	3985	3986	3987	3988	3989	3990	3991	3992	3993	3994	3995	3996	3997	3998	3999
FA0	4000	4001	4002	4003	4004	4005	4006	4007	4008	4009	4010	4011	4012	4013	4014	4015
FB0	4016	1017	1018	4019	4020	4021	4022	4023	4024	4025	4026	4027	4028	4029	4030	4031
FC0	4032	4033	4034	4035	4036	4037	4038	4039	4040	4041	4042	4043	4044	4045	4046	4047
FD0	40:8	4049	4050	4051	4052	4053	4054	4055	4056	4057	4058	4059	4060	4061	4062	4063
FE0	4064	4065	4066	4067	4068	4069	4070	4071	4072	4073	4074	4075	4076	4077	4078	4079
FF0	4080	4081	4082	4083	4084	4085	4086	4087	4088	4089	4090	4091	4092	4093	4094	4095

Index

Index

A

Antenna pattern	92
Arithmetic mean	59

B

BASIC statements and commands	230

C

Calculations, great circle	227
Capacitive-divider network	143
Chi-square evaluation	89
Combinations	57
Complex cosecant	191
cosine	183
cotangent	187
functions	17, 180
operations	14
secant	189
sine	181
tangent	185
Complex arc cosecant	204
cosine	195
cotangent	199
secant	201
sine	193
tangent	197
Complex hyperbolic cosecant	216
cosine	209
cotangent	212
functions	207
secant	214
sine	207
tangent	210
Compound interest	31
Conversion,	

hexadecimal-decimal	237
Conversion from base 10	21
Conversion to base 10	19

D

Decimal-hexadecimal conversion	237

E

Electronics	91
Exponential curve fit	81

F

Factorial	87
Finance	30
Future value	37

G

Gamma match	98
Geometric mean	61
Geometry	153
Great circle calculations	227
Grouped data	71
Grouped data mean	65

H

Hexadecimal-decimal conversion	237
Hyperbolic cosecant	164
cosine	157
cosine graph	158
cotangent	162
secant	166
sine	154
sine graph	155
tangent	161
Harmonic mean	63

I

Inverse hyperbolic cosine 170
  cosine graph 171
  cotangent 174, 178
  contangent graph 175, 179
  functions 168
  secant 176
  secant graph 177
  sine 168
  sine graph 169
  tangent 172
  tangent graph 173
Interest rate 35

L

Linear regression 73
Loan 48
  amount 50
  balance 45
Logrithmic curve fit 78

M

Matching networks 128
Microstrip 150
Minimum-loss pad 123
Monthly loan payment 43

N

Network A 128
  B 132
  C 135
  D 139
New base conversion 23
Number of payments 41, 48
Numbers 11
Numerical integration 26

O

Omega match 107

P

Parallel/series
  conversions 125
Permutations 55
Pi-pad 120
Polar/rectangular
  conversion 12
Powers of two 236

R

Required payment 39

S

Savings 41
Series matching section 146
Simultaneous equations 24
Sinking fund 52
Standard deviation 69, 71
Statements and
  commands, BASIC 230
Statistics 54

T

T-pad 115
Triangles 218
  three sides 221
  two angles with
    opposite side 223
  two sides with
    included angle 225
  two sides with non-
    included angle 218
Two, powers of 236

U

Ungrouped data 69

Y

Years of interest 33